VEGAN BODYB COOKBOOK

100 high protein recipes for a strong body while maintaining health, vitality and energy

Table of Contents

Introduction

When I started out with fitness a couple of years ago, I tried to consume as much information as possible about nutrition, fitness, workout routines and much more. When it comes to nutrition, the advice I could find was pretty much always the same: Take care of your protein intake. All other aspects were rather secondary, as protein is very important for building muscles.

When I turned vegan, I was very worried about the difficulty of reaching my protein intake goals on a vegan diet. After doing a lot of research, I realised that these two things are in no way contradictory: with the right knowledge and recipes, it no problem at all to eat high-protein vegan meals that are also delicious. In this book, I have collected the best high protein recipes that I came across, which are also delicious and easy to make.

The cookbook will provide you with inspiration for vegan foods with plenty of protein. I hope it will open your eyes to the world of vegan fitness nutrition and that a plant-based diet is not contradictory to bodybuilding and being strong and in shape.

The book will change your perception on protein intake, the specific required amounts and guide you towards various sources of vegan proteins and how these can be effectively utilized to achieve the ideal muscle build.

Enjoy!

PART 1: Vegan Bodybuilding – Getting Started

"You can't get enough protein as a vegan"

"Oh, you are vegan...where do you get your proteins from?"

If you are a vegan, you probably heard this sentence a million times. There is a common misconception about veganism spread in people's minds: You can't get enough protein as a vegan. There are several perceptions that influence this view.

One of them is the often contradictory opinion on how much protein is actually required for effective bodybuilding. The second is the protein source - animal protein or plant protein? If you are more advanced you also care about the exact amino acid intakes and if you get enough of all the essential ones.

We need to change our view on the amount of protein in foods. What is the scale in which protein in food is measured? Let's compare two foods in their protein content: 100 grams of chicken contain about 25 grams of protein, while 100 grams of broccoli only contain 2.8 grams of protein.

Is this a fair comparison? At the end of the day, nobody measures their food intake in weight. Your body measures the food in calories. I have never heard anyone say "I ate 850 grams of food today". People say "I ate 2500 kcal today". This is the reference that should be used when comparing protein contents of foods. Let's get back to broccoli and chicken. Chicken contains 10,3 grams of protein per 100 kcal while broccoli contains about 8,2 grams of protein per 100 kcal. Chicken still contains more, but the difference is really small. Plant based foods are way less calorie dense than animal foods, and the amount of vegetables, beans and legumes you can eat is way more than animal foods. This is what people neglect when thinking about how much protein you can acquire when eating a plant based diet. Furthermore, there are actually a lot of vegan foods with high protein contents such as beans, legumes, tofu, tempeh, seitan, broccoli and many more.

All the proteins your body needs can be obtained from a fully plant-based diet. A healthy mixture is the key to success. Many people end up with their few recipes that they keep repeating over and over again. Even if those foods and recipes are healthy, they are still repetitive and make it harder to acquire all the essential micro-nutrients, amino acids and minerals. Keep mixing in different vegetables. Be open and try out new stuff. Nature has incorporated enough variety in healthy plants and fruits to nourish us with all we need. Use it and don't end up eating the same things over and over again.

If you are serious about being on a vegan diet while bodybuilding, you need to be aware which foods contain which nutrients. This makes it easier for you to see and realize "Oh, I did not have a lot of leafy greens lately, maybe that would be good to get some iron and zinc in". You can mix your foods accordingly, but a general understanding is essential. Here is a tiny list of foods which contain nutrients that are usually advocated by media as "hard to get as a vegan":

✓　　**Iron:** Spinach, tomatoes, bell pepper, beans, berries, and whole cereals contain ample amounts of iron.
✓　　**Zinc:** Leafy vegetables and greens, beetroot, peas, whole-grain bread, and nuts.
✓　　**Vitamin B12:** Plant based milks, seaweeds, supplements.
✓　　**Omega 3 fatty acids:** Flax seeds, chia seeds, soybeans and especially walnuts.

✓   **Vitamin D:** Oranges, mushrooms, soy milk and cereals contain a fairly large amount of Vitamin D.

✓   **Calcium:** Broccoli, almonds, chickpeas, black beans, turnip greens, and soybeans etc.

Another wrong assumption is that plant protein is inferior to animal protein. Animal and plant protein are both essentially composed of amino acids and these are no different from one another.

The difference lies in the fact that while animal proteins are alone sufficient in terms of protein value, the plant products may not necessarily contain the essential amino acids in the same ratio. This is, however, a not a big problem because you enjoy a variety of meals during a day and thus in form of one food or another, will manage to reach your protein goals.

While there isn't any striking difference between the two except in terms of high or low ratios of amino acids, the real problem arises when you compare what else accompanies the proteins. While animal food is high in protein, it is at the same time very high in fats, cholesterol and calories.

The same is not true for plant foods. These types of foods are effective in battling heart-related disorders, hypertension, diabetes, bad cholesterol, gallbladder stones, kidney stones, fatty liver, high uric acid, high triglycerides, and many more problems. These are also much safer to consume and healthy at the same time.

So, if you are an aspiring vegan bodybuilder, the key to your success is consuming a lot of both complete and incomplete plant protein foods and simultaneously consuming a lot of fiber, vitamins, and minerals. Little amounts of fat and carbohydrates are also required by your body for growth.

"You need a lot of protein to build muscles"

People are generally unaware of their daily protein need and they end up consuming double the actual requirement. This is especially true for bodybuilders who overload their diet with proteins and neglect their needs for vitamins and minerals.

While there is no doubt that protein is a very important factor when building muscles, there is a huge misconception about the exact amount. Many people advocate "the more protein the better". This is obviously an overstatement and can actually backfire. Too much protein intake can actually harm the body and cause many health problems. The question remaining is "How much protein is actually needed?". The dietary guidelines are usually around 50 grams of protein a day - for non-athletes. This is not enough for the purpose of bodybuilding. In the fitness community, also many claim that 2-3 grams of protein per kilogram of bodyweight.

There is an abundance of studies proposing many different outcomes and it is hard to keep an overview about which study is actually representing the truth. But for the purposes of building muscles 1.2-1.5 grams of protein per kilogram of bodyweight is more than sufficient. If you keep having problems with reaching this daily protein goal, you can always settle for plant based protein powders with rich amino acids like peas protein or rice proteins, we will also use some recipes with plant based protein powders in the recipes.

Being healthy vs. bulking up

Unfortunately, being healthy and having a perfectly bulked up body is not equivalent. Many bodybuilders only care about their protein intake and their other macronutrients. IIFYM (If it fits your macros) is one of the dietary guidelines proposed by the media. Everyone needs to be certain about their priorities. I personally decided that a healthy body is more important than a good looking body. You may look amazing, lean, ripped, bulked - but your body is crying for help. Be aware of the fact that health comes from a variety of foods and nutrients. You can't reduce health to just the protein intake. The next time somebody asks you if you get enough protein, ask them if they get enough fiber or magnesium.

Plant based protein sources

There are not one but plenty of ways for you to get sufficient protein nourishment and that too without any animal slaughter. Abundant in all nutrients, plant foods are a healthy substitute to meat.

Here is a list of few protein-rich vegan foods than you can add to your diet chart:

> **SOY:** It contains an extremely important amino acid, glutamine, which reduces the harmful effects caused by stress and anxiety. Soy has anti-cancerous properties and also helps in reducing the risk associated with hypertension.

It is readily available in the market as regular soybean, powdered and tinned form. You can use soy milk, soy chunks, also known as meat extenders, are very nutritious and protein-rich. Soy sauce is used in many dishes as an important ingredient. A serving of 100 ml of soya sauce contains 10.51g of proteins.

➤ **LENTILS:** Proteins account to almost 26% of total lentil calories (remember our new view on protein content!). Consuming lentils keeps your body healthy in a number of ways. These are good for your heart, digestive track, and blood sugar. This extensively energy rich food burns slowly and thus keeps releasing energy for longer hours.

Lentils are nutritious because they not only contain proteins but fiber, calcium, phosphorous, iron and few other nutrients too. The lentil protein comes under the category of incomplete protein because it lacks a few amino acids. Thus, you can consume it in combination with other foods to have a wholesome protein diet.

➤ **TOFU:** Tofu is the vegetarian's curd. It is made by condensing soya milk and then forming either soft or hard textured blocks from the resulting curd. These are very high in protein content and you can use these in both savory dishes and desserts.

About 10.7g per 100g of tofu consists of proteins and one block contains approximately 180 calories. The soy protein is said be a cholesterol reducing agent, prevents osteoporosis, enhances kidney function, prevents liver dysfunction and minimizes heart diseases. It carries lesser calories and is an important source of iron, calcium, and magnesium along with protein.

➤ **BEANS AND LEGUMES:** One of the richest sources of protein, beans and legumes are strong antioxidants too. Almost 8 grams of protein are served on your plate per half a cup of cooked beans. These are also rich in vitamins and minerals. A cup of cooked black beans contains not more than 115kcl.

As it contains complex carbohydrates, it burn slowly and thus prevents sudden rise in your blood sugar level and also provides energy to your body day long.

Beans are helpful in restoring the bone strength, protecting the heart, maintaining optimum blood sugar level, and preventing cancer.

➤ **ALMONDS (NUTS IN GENERAL):** Almonds contain 21g of protein per 100 grams which means that consuming a handful of almonds provides you with approximately 2.5grams of proteins.

As almonds come under the category of incomplete proteins, they are deficient in a few amino acids. Thus, munching a few almonds along with other plant based proteins is a good and healthy idea.

Almonds are also rich sources of Vitamin E and magnesium. These help you to keep your blood pressure, cholesterol and blood sugar levels under control. After consuming a handful of almonds you feel less hungry and thus the overall calorie intake decreases.

➤ **QUINOA:** Quinoa is a gluten-free seed-type grain that is high in protein, magnesium, iron, riboflavin and antioxidants. A cup of cooked quinoa contains as many as 8 grams of protein. This grain contains almost double the fiber as any other grain.

It is a complete protein and a serving of quinoa provides your body with all the nine essential amino acids. There are some important plant compounds present in quinoa that give it anti-viral, anti-cancer and anti-inflammatory properties.

Consuming quinoa can help you to fight hypertension, reduce blood sugar and bad cholesterol and gives you a sense of fullness.

> **HEMP SEEDS:** Though hemp seeds are not complete proteins, when you consume these along other proteins, you can meet your optimum protein requirement. These contain almost 31.5 grams of protein per 100 grams.

The highly fibrous seeds are very useful for healthy digestion. Unlike many plant products, hemp seeds are rich in omega 3 fatty acids and Vitamin E. These also contain important minerals like magnesium and iron.

Hemp seeds are extremely effective for brain development due to omega 3 fatty acids. These are good for a healthy heart, stable blood pressure and blood sugar and other health issues.

> **DRIED PEAS:** The young sprouts that generate from the dried peas are an amazing source of protein. Approximately 11grams of protein are present in half a cup of dried peas.

Dried peas are also high in vitamin B complex and are rich sources of minerals like iron, potassium, magnesium, Vitamin K and C, and phosphorous. These are very healthy to consume as they contain fewer calories and almost no fat content.

As these are fiber filled, they are good for the digestive track. These are also known to be effective for the heart health, stabilizing blood pressure and much more.

Apart from the above mentioned, there are many more protein rich food choices available at your disposal. The choice of food that you can consider depends on your food preferences, likes and dislikes.

Thus we may conclude that veganism is not only being more vary of the animal rights, it is also very ecology friendly. At the same time, it reduces the harm that otherwise would be caused to us due to the consumption of animal protein like fluctuating levels of uric acid, bad cholesterol, diabetes, cancer, hypertension, heart problems and much more.

PART 2: High protein recipes

Breakfast Recipes

Peanut Butter Banana Quinoa Bowl

Preparation time: 15 minutes

Cooking time: 15 minutes

Serve: 1

Ingredients:

- 175ml unsweetened soy milk
- 85g uncooked quinoa
- ½ teaspoon Ceylon cinnamon
- 10g chia seeds
- 30g organic peanut butter
- 30ml unsweetened almond milk
- 10g raw cocoa powder
- 5 drops liquid stevia
- 1 small banana, peeled, sliced

Instructions:

1. In a saucepan, bring soy milk, quinoa, and Ceylon cinnamon to a boil.
2. Reduce heat and simmer 15 minutes.
3. Remove from the heat and stir in Chia seeds. Cover the saucepan with lid and place aside for 15 minutes.
4. In the meantime, microwave peanut butter and almond milk for 30 seconds on high. Remove and stir until runny. Repeat the process if needed.
5. Stir in raw cocoa powder and Stevia.
6. To serve; fluff the quinoa with fork and transfer in a bowl.
7. Top with sliced banana.
8. Drizzle the quinoa with peanut butter.
9. Serve.

Nutritional info per serving:

- Calories 718
- Total Fat 29.6g
- Total Carbohydrate 90.3g
- Dietary Fiber 17.5g
- Total Sugars 14.5g
- Protein 30.4g

Orange Pumpkin Pancakes

Preparation time: 10 minutes

Cooking time: 15 minutes

Serve: 4

Ingredients:

- 10g ground flax meal
- 45ml water
- 235ml unsweetened soy milk
- 15ml lemon juice
- 60g buckwheat flour
- 60g all-purpose flour
- 8g baking powder, aluminum-free
- 2 teaspoons finely grated orange zest
- 25g white chia seeds
- 120g organic pumpkin puree (or just bake the pumpkin and puree the flesh)
- 30ml melted and cooled coconut oil
- 5ml vanilla paste
- 30ml pure maple syrup

Instructions:

1. Combine ground flax meal with water in a small bowl. Place aside for 10 minutes.
2. Combine almond milk and cider vinegar in a medium bowl. Place aside for 5 minutes.
3. In a separate large bowl, combine buckwheat flour, all-purpose flour, baking powder, orange zest, and chia seeds.
4. Pour in almond milk, along with pumpkin puree, coconut oil, vanilla, and maple syrup.
5. Whisk together until you have a smooth batter.
6. Heat large non-stick skillet over medium-high heat. Brush the skillet gently with some coconut oil.
7. Pour 60ml of batter into skillet. Cook the pancake for 1 minute, or until bubbles appear on the surface.

8. Lift the pancake gently with a spatula and flip.
9. Cook 1 ½ minutes more. Slide the pancake onto a plate. Repeat with the remaining batter.
10. Serve warm.

Nutritional info per serving:

- Calories 301
- Total Fat 12.6g
- Total Carbohydrate 41.7g
- Dietary Fiber 7.2g
- Total Sugars 9.9g
- Protein 8.1g

Sweet Potato slices with Fruits

Preparation time: 10 minutes

Cooking time: 10 minutes

Serve: 2

Ingredients:

The base:

- 1 sweet potato

Topping:

- 60g organic peanut butter
- 30ml pure maple syrup
- 4 dried apricots, sliced
- 30g fresh raspberries

Instructions:

1. Peel and cut sweet potato into ½ cm thick slices.
2. Place the potato slices in a toaster on high for 5 minutes. Toast your sweet potatoes TWICE.
3. Arrange sweet potato slices onto a plate.
4. Spread the peanut butter over sweet potato slices.
5. Drizzle the maple syrup over the butter.
6. Top each slice with an equal amount of sliced apricots and raspberries.
7. Serve.

Nutritional info per serving:

- Calories 300
- Total Fat 16.9g
- Total Carbohydrate 32.1g
- Dietary Fiber 6.2g
- Total Sugars 17.7g
- Protein 10.3g

Breakfast Oat Brownies

Preparation time: 10 minutes

Cooking time: 40 minutes

Serve: 10 slices (2 per serving)

Ingredients:

- 180g old-fashioned rolled oats
- 80g peanut flour
- 30g chickpea flour
- 25g flax seeds meal
- 5g baking powder, aluminum-free
- ½ teaspoon baking soda
- 5ml vanilla paste
- 460ml unsweetened vanilla soy milk
- 80g organic applesauce
- 55g organic pumpkin puree
- 45g organic peanut butter
- 5ml liquid stevia extract
- 25g slivered almonds

Instructions:

1. Preheat oven to 180C/350F.
2. Line 18cm baking pan with parchment paper, leaving overhanging sides.
3. In a large bowl, combine oats, peanut flour, chickpea flour, flax seeds, baking powder, and baking soda.
4. In a separate bowl, whisk together vanilla paste, soy milk, applesauce. Pumpkin puree, peanut butter, and stevia.
5. Fold the liquid ingredients into dry ones and stir until incorporated.
6. Pour the batter into the prepared baking pan.
7. Sprinkle evenly with slivered almonds.
8. Bake the oat brownies for 40 minutes.
9. Remove from the oven and place aside to cool.
10. Slice and serve.

Nutritional info per serving:

- Calories 309
- Total Fat 15.3g
- Total Carbohydrate 32.2g
- Dietary Fiber 9.2g
- Total Sugars 9.1g
- Protein 13.7g

Spinach Tofu Scramble with Sour Cream

Preparation time: 10 minutes

Cooking time: 15 minutes

Serve: 2

Ingredients:

Sour cream:

- 75g raw cashews, soaked overnight
- 30ml lemon juice
- 5g nutritional yeast
- 60ml water
- 1 good pinch salt

Tofu scramble:

- 15ml olive oil
- 1 small onion, diced
- 1 clove garlic, minced
- 400 firm tofu, pressed, crumbled
- ½ teaspoon ground cumin
- ½ teaspoon curry powder
- ½ teaspoon turmeric
- 2 tomatoes, diced
- 30g baby spinach
- Salt, to taste

Instructions:

1. Make the cashew sour cream; rinse and drain soaked cashews.
2. Place the cashews, lemon juice, nutritional yeast, water, and salt in a food processor.
3. Blend on high until smooth, for 5-6 minutes.
4. Transfer to a bowl and place aside.
5. Make the tofu scramble; heat olive oil in a skillet.
6. Add onion and cook 5 minutes over medium-high.

7. Add garlic, and cook stirring, for 1 minute.
8. Add crumbled tofu, and stir to coat with oil.
9. Add the cumin, curry, and turmeric. Cook the tofu for 2 minutes.
10. Add the tomatoes and cook for 2 minutes.
11. Add spinach and cook, tossing until completely wilted, about 1 minute.
12. Transfer tofu scramble on the plate.
13. Top with a sour cream and serve.

Nutritional info per serving:

- Calories 411
- Total Fat 26.5g
- Total Carbohydrate 23.1g
- Dietary Fiber 5.9g
- Total Sugars 6.3g
- Protein 25g

Overnight Chia Oats

Preparation time: 15minutes + inactive time

Cooking time: 20 minutes

Serve: 4

Ingredients:

- 470ml full-fat soy milk
- 90g old-fashioned rolled oats
- 40g chia seeds
- 15ml pure maple syrup
- 25g crushed pistachios

Blackberry Jam:

- 500g blackberries
- 45ml pure maple syrup
- 30ml water
- 45g chia seeds
- 15ml lemon juice

Instructions:

1. Make the oats; in a large bowl, combine soy milk, oats, chia seeds, and maple syrup.
2. Cover and refrigerate overnight.
3. Make the jam; combine blackberries, maple syrup, and water in a saucepan.
4. Simmer over medium heat for 10 minutes.
5. Add the chia seeds and simmer the blackberries for 10 minutes.
6. Remove from heat and stir in lemon juice. Mash the blackberries with a fork and place aside to cool.
7. Assemble; divide the oatmeal among four serving bowls.
8. Top with each bowl blackberry jam.
9. Sprinkle with pistachios before serving.

Nutritional info per serving:

- Calories 362
- Total Fat 13.4g
- Total Carbohydrate 52.6g
- Dietary Fiber 17.4g
- Total Sugars 24.6g
- Protein 12.4g

Mexican Breakfast

Preparation time: 10 minutes

Cooking time: 10 minutes

Serve: 4

Ingredients:

- 170g cherry tomatoes, halved
- 1 small red onion, chopped
- 25ml lime juice
- 50ml olive oil
- 1 clove garlic, minced
- 1 teaspoon red chili flakes
- 1 teaspoon ground cumin
- 700g can black beans* (or cooked beans), rinsed
- 4 slices whole-grain bread
- 1 avocado, peeled, pitted
- Salt, to taste

Instructions:

1. Combine tomatoes, onion, lime juice, and 15ml olive oil in a bowl.
2. Season to taste and place aside.
3. Heat 2 tablespoons olive oil in a skillet.
4. Add onion and cook 4 minutes over medium-high heat.
5. Add garlic and cook stirring for 1 minute.
6. Add red chili flakes and cumin. Cook for 30 seconds.
7. Add beans and cook tossing gently for 2 minutes.
8. Stir in ¾ of the tomato mixture and season to taste.
9. Remove from heat.
10. Slice the avocado very thinly.
11. Spread the beans mixture over bread slices. Top with remaining tomato and sliced avocado.
12. Serve.

Nutritional info per serving:

- Calories 476
- Total Fat 21.9g
- Total Carbohydrate 52.4g
- Dietary Fiber 19.5g
- Total Sugars 5.3g
- Protein 17.1g

Amaranth Quinoa porridge

Preparation time: 5 minutes

Cooking time: 35 minutes

Serve: 2

Ingredients:

- 85g quinoa
- 70g amaranth
- 460ml water
- 115ml unsweetened soy milk
- ½ teaspoon vanilla paste
- 15g almond butter
- 30ml pure maple syrup
- 10g raw pumpkin seeds
- 10g pomegranate seeds

Instructions:

1. Combine quinoa, amaranth, and water.
2. Bring to a boil over medium-high heat.
3. Reduce heat and simmer the grains, stirring occasionally, for 20 minutes.
4. Stir in milk and maple syrup.
5. Simmer for 6-7 minutes. Remove from the heat and stir in vanilla, and almond butter.
6. Allow the mixture to stand for 5 minutes.
7. Divide the porridge between two bowls.
8. Top with pumpkin seeds and pomegranate seeds.
9. Serve.

Nutritional info per serving:

- Calories 474
- Total Fat 13.3g
- Total Carbohydrate 73.2g
- Dietary Fiber 8.9g

- Total Sugars 10g
- Protein 17.8g

Cacao Lentil Muffins

Preparation time: 10 minutes

Cooking time: 15 minutes

Serve: 12 muffins (2 per serving)

Ingredients:

- 195g cooked red lentils
- 50ml melted coconut oil
- 45ml pure maple syrup
- 60ml unsweetened almond milk
- 60ml water
- 60g raw cocoa powder
- 120g whole-wheat flour
- 20g peanut flour
- 10g baking powder, aluminum-free
- 70g Vegan chocolate chips

Instructions:

1. Preheat oven to 200C/400F.
2. Line 12-hole muffin tin with paper cases.
3. Place the cooked red lentils in a food blender. Blend on high until smooth.
4. Transfer the lentils puree into a large bowl.
5. Stir in coconut oil, maple syrup, almond milk, and water.
6. In a separate bowl, whisk cocoa powder, whole-wheat flour, peanut flour, and baking powder.
7. Fold in liquid ingredients and stir until just combined.
8. Add chocolate chips and stir until incorporated.
9. Divide the batter among 12 paper cases.
10. Tap the muffin tin gently onto the kitchen counter to remove air.
11. Bake the muffins for 15 minutes.
12. Cool muffins on a wire rack.
13. Serve.

Nutritional info per serving:

- Calories 372
- Total Fat 13.5g
- Total Carbohydrate 52.7g
- Dietary Fiber 12.9g
- Total Sugars 13g
- Protein 13.7g

Chickpea Crepes with Mushrooms and Spinach

Preparation time: 20 minutes + inactive time

Cooking time: 15 minutes

Serve: 4

Ingredients:

Crepes:

- 140g chickpea flour
- 30g peanut flour
- 5g nutritional yeast
- 5g curry powder
- 350ml water
- Salt, to taste

Filling:

- 10ml olive oil
- 4 portabella mushroom caps, thinly sliced
- 1 onion, thinly sliced
- 30g baby spinach
- Salt, and pepper, to taste

Vegan mayo:

- 60ml aquafaba
- 1/8 teaspoon cream of tartar
- ¼ teaspoon dry mustard powder
- 15ml lemon juice
- 5ml raw cider vinegar
- 15ml maple syrup
- 170ml avocado oil
- Salt, to taste

Instructions:

1. Make the mayo; combine aquafaba, cream of tartar, mustard powder. Lemon juice, cider vinegar, and maple syrup in a bowl.
2. Beat with a hand mixer for 30 seconds.
3. Set the mixer to the highest speed. Drizzle in avocado oil and beat for 10 minutes or until you have a mixture that resembles mayonnaise.
4. Of you want paler (in the color mayo) add more lemon juice.
5. Season with salt and refrigerate for 1 hour.
6. Make the crepes; combine chickpea flour, peanut flour, nutritional yeast, curry powder, water, and salt to taste in a food blender.
7. Blend until smooth.
8. Heat large non-stick skillet over medium-high heat. Spray the skillet with some cooking oil.
9. Pour ¼ cup of the batter into skillet and with a swirl motion distribute batter all over the skillet bottom.
10. Cook the crepe for 1 minute per side. Slide the crepe onto a plate and keep warm.
11. Make the filling; heat olive oil in a skillet over medium-high heat.
12. Add mushrooms and onion and cook for 6-8 minutes.
13. Add spinach and toss until wilted, for 1 minute.
14. Season with salt and pepper and transfer into a large bowl.
15. Fold in prepared vegan mayo.
16. Spread the prepared mixture over chickpea crepes. Fold gently and serve.

Nutritional info per serving:

- Calories 428
- Total Fat 13.3g
- Total Carbohydrate 60.3g
- Dietary Fiber 18.5g
- Total Sugars 13.2g
- Protein 22.6g

Goji Breakfast Bowl

Preparation time: 10 minutes

Serve: 2

Ingredients:

- 15g chia seeds
- 10g buckwheat
- 15g hemp seeds
- 20g Goji berries
- 235mml vanilla soy milk

Instructions:

1. Combine chia, buckwheat, hemp seeds, and Goji berries in a bowl.
2. Heat soy milk in a saucepan until start to simmer.
3. Pour the milk over "cereals".
4. Allow the cereals to stand for 5 minutes.
5. Serve.

Nutritional info per serving:

- Calories 339
- Total Fat 14.3g
- Total Carbohydrate 41.8g
- Dietary Fiber 10.5g
- Total Sugars 20g
- Protein 13.1g

Breakfast Berry Parfait

Preparation time: 10 minutes

Serve: 1

Ingredients:

- 250g soy yogurt
- 10g wheat germ
- 40g raspberries
- 40g blackberries
- 30ml maple syrup
- 10g slivered almonds

Instructions:

1. Pour 1/3 of soy yogurt in a parfait glass.
2. Top with raspberries and 1 tablespoon wheat germ.
3. Repeat layer with blackberries and remaining wheat germ.
4. Finish with soy yogurt.
5. Drizzle the parfait with maple syrup and sprinkle with almonds.
6. Serve.

Nutritional info per serving:

- Calories 327
- Total Fat 9.4g
- Total Carbohydrate 48.7g
- Dietary Fiber 8.4g
- Total Sugars 29.3g
- Protein 15.6g

Mini Tofu Frittatas

Preparation time: 15 minutes

Cooking time: 25 minutes

Serve: 12 mini frittatas (3 per serving)

Ingredients:

- 450g firm tofu, drained
- 115ml soy milk
- 5g mild curry powder
- 15ml olive oil
- 20g chopped scallions
- 80g corn kernels, fresh
- 140g cherry tomatoes, quartered
- 75g baby spinach
- Salt and pepper, to taste

Pesto for serving:

- 15g fresh basil
- 10g walnuts
- 1 clove garlic, peeled
- 10g lemon juice
- 5g nutritional yeast
- 20ml olive oil
- 30ml water
- Salt, to taste

Instructions:

1. Make the frittatas; Preheat oven to 180C/350F.
2. Line 12-hole mini muffin pan with paper cases.
3. Combine tofu, soy milk, and curry powder in a food blender. Blend until smooth.
4. Heat olive oil in a skillet.
5. Add scallions and cook 3 minutes.
6. Add corn and tomatoes. Cook 2 minutes.

7. Add spinach, and cook stirring for 1 minute. Season to taste.
8. Stir the veggies into tofu mixture.
9. Divide the tofu-vegetable mixture among 12 paper cases.
10. Bake the frittata for 25 minutes.
11. In the meantime, make the pesto; combine basil, walnuts, lemon juice, and nutritional yeast in a food processor.
12. Process until smooth.
13. Add olive oil and process until smooth.
14. Scrape down the sides and add water. Process until creamy.
15. To serve; remove frittatas from the oven. Cool on a wire rack.
16. Remove the frittatas from the muffin tin. Top each with pesto.
17. Serve.

Nutritional info per serving:

- Calories 220
- Total Fat 14.2g
- Total Carbohydrate 13.5g
- Dietary Fiber 4.5g
- Total Sugars 4g
- Protein 15g

Brownie Pancakes

Preparation time: 10 minutes

Cooking time: 5 minutes

Serve: 2

Ingredients:

- 35g cooked black beans
- 30g all-purpose flour
- 25g peanut flour
- 25g raw cocoa powder
- 5g baking powder, aluminum free
- 15ml pure maple sugar
- 60g unsweetened soy milk
- 35g organic applesauce
- ½ teaspoon vanilla paste
- 10g crushed almonds

Instructions:

1. Combine cooked black beans, all-purpose flour, peanut flour, cocoa powder, and baking powder in a bowl.
2. In a separate bowl, whisk maple syrup, soy milk, applesauce, and vanilla.
3. Fold liquid ingredients into dry and whisk until smooth. You can also toss ingredients into a food blender and blend.
4. Heat large non-stick skillet over medium-high heat. Spray the skillet with some cooking oil.
5. Pour ¼ cup of batter into skillet. Sprinkle with some almonds.
6. Cook the pancakes on each side for 1 ½ - 2 minutes.
7. Serve warm, drizzled with desired syrup.

Nutritional info per serving:

- Calories 339
- Total Fat 9.5g
- Total Carbohydrate 46.8g

- Dietary Fiber 11.2g
- Total Sugars 6.5g
- Protein 26.5g

Chickpea Muffin Quiche

Preparation time: 15 minutes

Cooking time: 65 minutes

Serve: 12 muffins (3 per serving)

Ingredients:

- 280g sweet potato, peeled, cut into ¼-inch cubes
- 15ml olive oil
- 90g chickpea flour
- 10g nutritional yeast
- 460ml water
- 30g spinach
- 40g chestnut mushrooms, sliced
- 35g shiitake mushrooms, chopped
- Salt and pepper, to taste

Instructions:

1. Heat oven to 200C/425F.
2. Grease 12-hole muffin with some oil.
3. Line a baking sheet with baking paper.
4. Toss the sweet potato cubes with olive oil, salt, and pepper, on a baking sheet.
5. Roast the sweet potato for 20 minutes.
6. Remove the sweet potatoes from the oven and place aside. Reduce oven heat to 350F.
7. In the meantime, whisk chickpea flour, nutritional yeast, and 235ml water in a bowl. Season to taste with salt.
8. Bring remaining water to a simmer over medium-high heat.
9. Whisk in the chickpea flour mixture and reduce heat to low.
10. Cook the chickpea stirring constantly flour for 6 minutes or until thickened.
11. Remove from the heat and stir in baby spinach, mushrooms, and sweet potatoes.
12. Divide the mixture among muffin tin.

13. Place the muffin tin in the oven. Bake the quiche muffins for 25-30 minutes.
14. Remove from the oven and cool on a wire rack.
15. Serve while still warm.

Nutritional info per serving:

- Calories 247
- Total Fat 6.1g
- Total Carbohydrate 36.2g
- Dietary Fiber 8.3g
- Total Sugars 2.8g
- Protein 14.6g

Quinoa Pancake with Apricot

Preparation time: 10 minutes + inactive time

Cooking time: 25 minutes

Serve: 4

Ingredients:

- 115ml vanilla soy milk
- 120g apple sauce
- 15ml lemon juice
- 5g baking soda
- 30ml pure maple syrup
- 190g quinoa flour

Sauce:

- 60g dried apricots
- 5ml lemon juice
- 15ml maple syrup
- 170ml water

Instructions:

1. Make the sauce; wash the apricots and soak in water for 1 hour.
2. Chop the apricots and place in a saucepan with lemon juice and maple syrup.
3. Cover the apricots with water and bring to a boil over medium-high heat.
4. Reduce heat and simmer the apricots for 12-15 minutes.
5. Remove from the heat and cool slightly before transfer into a food blender.
6. Blend the apricots until smooth. Place aside.
7. Make the pancakes; in a large bowl, beat soy milk, applesauce, lemon juice, and maple syrup.
8. Sift in quinoa flour and baking soda.
9. Stir until you have a smooth batter.

10. Heat large skillet over medium-high heat. Spray the skillet with some cooking oil.
11. Pour ¼ cup of the batter into skillet.
12. Cook the pancakes for 2 minutes per side.
13. Serve pancakes with apricot sauce.

Nutritional info per serving:

- Calories 273
- Total Fat 3g
- Total Carbohydrate 51.6g
- Dietary Fiber 5.2g
- Total Sugars 19g
- Protein 7.9g

Artichoke Spinach Squares

Preparation time: 10 minutes

Cooking time: 30 minutes

Serve: 8 squares, (2 per serving)

Ingredients:

- 340g artichoke hearts, marinated in water, drained
- 15ml olive oil
- 1 small onion, diced
- 1 clove garlic, minced
- 250g silken tofu
- 30ml unsweetened soy milk
- 40g almond meal
- 60g baby spinach
- Salt and pepper, to taste
- 1/8 teaspoon dried oregano

Instructions:

1. Preheat oven to 180C/350F.
2. Line 8-inch baking pan with parchment paper.
3. Drain artichokes and chop finely.
4. Heat olive oil in a skillet over medium-high heat.
5. Add onion and cook 4 minutes. Add garlic and cook 1 minute.
6. Add artichoke hearts and spinach. Cook 1 minute.
7. Remove from the heat and place aside to cool.
8. In the meantime, combine silken tofu, soy milk, salt, pepper, and oregano in a food blender.
9. Blend until smooth.
10. Stir in almond meal and artichoke mixture.
11. Pour the mixture into baking pan.
12. Bake for 25-30 minutes or until lightly browned.
13. Remove from the oven and cool 10 minutes.
14. Slice and serve.

Nutritional info per serving:

- Calories 183
- Total Fat 10.6g
- Total Carbohydrate 15.5g
- Dietary Fiber 6.7g
- Total Sugars 3.2g
- Protein 10.1g

Breakfast Blini with Black Lentil Caviar

Preparation time: 15 minutes + inactive time

Cooking time: 35 minutes

Serve: 4

Ingredients:

For the blinis:

- 170ml unsweetened soy milk
- 5g instant yeast
- 120g buckwheat flour
- 75g all-purpose flour
- 45ml aquafaba (chickpea water)
- Salt, to taste

Lentil Caviar:

- 15ml olive oil
- 1 carrot, grated
- 2 scallions, chopped
- 100g black lentils
- 235ml water
- 15ml balsamic vinegar
- Salt and pepper, to taste

Instructions:

1. Make the lentils; heat olive oil in a saucepot.
2. Add carrot and scallions. Cook 4 minutes over medium-high heat.
3. Add lentils and stir gently to coat with oil. Pour in water and bring to a boil.
4. Reduce heat and simmer lentils for 35 minutes or until tender.
5. Stir in balsamic vinegar and season to taste. Place aside.
6. Make the blinis; warm soy milk in a saucepan over medium heat.
7. In the meantime, whisk yeast with buckwheat flour, all-purpose flour, and salt to taste.

8. Gradually pour in warm milk until you have a smooth batter.
9. Beat aquafaba in a bowl until frothy. Fold the aquafaba into the batter.
10. Cover the batter with a clean cloth and place aside, at room temperature, for 1 hour.
11. Heat large skillet over medium-high heat. Coat the skillet with cooking spray.
12. Drop 1 tablespoon of batter into skillet. Gently distribute the batter, with a back of the spoon, just to create 2 ½ -inch circle.
13. Cook the blini for 1 minute per side.
14. Serve blinis with lentil caviar.
15. Garnish with some chopped coriander before serving.

Nutritional info per serving:

- Calories 340
- Total Fat 5.9g
- Total Carbohydrate 58.8g
- Dietary Fiber 12.5g
- Total Sugars 4.4g
- Protein 14.9g

Hemp Seed Banana Cereal

Preparation time: 10 minutes

Cooking time: 25 minutes

Serve: 4

Ingredients:

- 5g ground flax seeds
- 45ml water
- 70g almond meal
- 60g walnuts, chopped
- 80g hemp seeds
- 30g unsweetened coconut flakes
- 3 tablespoon coconut sugar
- 1 ½ tablespoons coconut oil, melted
- 1 teaspoon banana extract
- 460ml unsweetened almond milk, warmed

Instructions:

1. In a small bowl, combine flax seeds, and water. Place aside for 10 minutes.
2. Preheat oven to 150C/300F.
3. Line a large baking sheet with parchment paper.
4. Combine almond meal, walnuts, hemp seeds, coconut flakes, and coconut sugar, in a large bowl.
5. In a separate bowl, combine flax seeds mixture, with coconut oil, and banana extract.
6. Pour the flax seeds mixture into dry ingredients and stir to combine.
7. Spread the mixture onto baking sheet.
8. Bake the cereals for 25 minutes, stirring 2-3 times during the baking process.
9. Turn off the oven and allow the cereals to cool down for 10 minutes.
10. Serve with warmed almond milk.

Nutritional info per serving:

- Calories 495
- Total Fat 40.2g
- Total Carbohydrate 20.4g
- Dietary Fiber 5.3g
- Total Sugars 9.8g
- Protein 18.3g

Oatmeal Muffins

Preparation time: 10 minutes

Cooking time: 30 minutes

Serve: 12 muffins (2 per serving)

Ingredients:

- 2 ripe bananas, mashed
- 70g organic pumpkin puree
- 30ml pure maple syrup
- 270 quick-cooking rolled oats
- 5 dates, chopped
- 50g dried chopped apricots
- 15ml coconut oil
- 460ml unsweetened soy milk
- 5ml vanilla paste
- 12 cashew nuts

Instructions:

1. Preheat oven to 180C/350F.
2. Line 12-hole muffin tin with paper cases.
3. Combine banana, pumpkin puree, and maple syrup in a bowl.
4. Stir in oats, dates, apricots. And coconut oil.
5. Add soy milk, vanilla, and mix until fully combined.
6. Divide the mixture among prepared paper cases.
7. Tap the muffin tin onto the kitchen counter to remove any air captured in the batter.
8. Top each muffin with cashew nut.
9. Bake the muffins for 30 minutes.
10. Cool on a wire rack before serving.

Nutritional info per serving:

- Calories 292
- Total Fat 5.8g
- Total Carbohydrate 52.5g

- Dietary Fiber 6.9g
- Total Sugars 23.7g
- Protein 9g

Lunch Recipes

Potato Bean Quesadillas

Preparation time: 10 minutes

Cooking time: 10 minutes

Servings: 4

Ingredients:

- 4 whole-wheat tortillas
- 2 potatoes, boiled, cubed
- 200g refried beans
- 1 teaspoon chili powder
- ½ teaspoon dried oregano
- ¼ teaspoon garlic powder
- 120g spinach
- 1 onion, thinly sliced
- 2 cloves garlic, minced
- 30ml tamari sauce
- 45g nutritional yeast
- Salt and pepper, to taste

Instructions:

1. Heat a splash of olive oil in a skillet.
2. Add onion and cook over medium heat for 10 minutes, or until the onion is caramelized.
3. Add the garlic and cook 1 minute.
4. Add spinach and toss gently.
5. Add tamari sauce and cook 1 minutes.
6. Reheat the refried beans with nutritional yeast, chili, oregano, and garlic powder, in a microwave, on high for 1 minute.
7. Mash the potatoes and spread over tortilla.
8. Top the mashed potatoes with spinach mixture and refried beans.
9. Season to taste and place another tortilla on top.
10. Heat large skillet over medium-high heat.

11. Heat the tortilla until crispy. Flip and heat the other side.
12. Cut the tortilla in half and serve.

Nutritional info per serving:

- Calories 232
- Total Fat 2.1g
- Total Carbohydrate 44.2g
- Dietary Fiber 10.4g
- Total Sugars 3g
- Protein 12.4g

Lemon Pepper Pasta

Preparation time: 5 minutes

Cooking time: 20 minutes

Servings: 4

Ingredients:

- 300g pasta, any kind, without eggs
- 400ml unsweetened soy milk
- 100g soy cream cheese
- 45g blanched almonds
- 45g nutritional yeast
- 1 teaspoon lemon zest, finely grated
- ¼ teaspoon lemon pepper
- 30ml olive oil
- 2 clove garlic, minced
- 5 capers, rinsed, chopped
- 10g parsley, chopped

Instructions:

1. Cook the pasta, according to the package directions, in a pot filled with salted boiling water.
2. Strain the pasta and reserve 230ml cooking liquid.
3. Combine soy milk, soy cheese, almonds, nutritional yeast, lemon zest, and pepper lemon in a food blender.
4. Blend until smooth. Place aside.
5. Heat olive oil in a skillet.
6. Add the garlic, and cook until very fragrant, for 1 minute.
7. Pour in the soy milk mixture and reserved pasta cooking liquid.
8. Bring to a boil, and reduce heat.
9. Stir in chopped capers and simmer 6-8 minutes or until creamy. Remove from the heat and stir in cooked pasta.
10. Toss the pasta gently to coat with the sauce.
11. Serve pasta, garnished with chopped parsley.

Nutritional info per serving:

- Calories 489
- Total Fat 23g
- Total Carbohydrate 53.5g
- Dietary Fiber 5.9g
- Total Sugars 2.4g
- Protein 20.4g

Lentils salad with Lemon Tahini Dressing

Preparation time: 10 minutes

Cooking time: 30 minutes

Servings: 4

Ingredients:

- 225g green lentils, picked, rinsed
- 1 clove garlic, minced
- ¼ teaspoon ground cumin
- 5ml olive oil
- 1 red onion, finely diced
- 75g dried apricots, chopped
- 1 small red bell pepper, seeded, chopped
- 1 small green bell pepper, seeded, chopped
- 1 small yellow bell pepper, seeded, chopped
- 1 small cucumber, diced
- 20g sunflower seeds
- Salt and pepper, to taste

Lemon dressing:

- 1 lemon, juiced
- 30g tahini
- 5g chopped coriander
- Salt, to taste

Instructions:

1. Place rinsed lentils in a saucepan.
2. Add enough water to cover.
3. Bring to a boil and skim off any foam. Add garlic and cumin.
4. Reduce heat and simmer the lentils for 30 minutes.
5. In the meantime, make the dressing by combining all the ingredients together.
6. Heat olive oil in a skillet. Add onion and bell peppers. Cook stirring over medium-high heat for 5 minutes.

7. Remove from the heat.
8. Drain the lentils and toss in a large bowl with the cooked vegetables, apricots, cucumber, and sunflower seeds. Season to taste.
9. Drizzle with dressing and serve.

Nutritional info per serving:

- Calories 318
- Total Fat 7g
- Total Carbohydrate 49.2g
- Dietary Fiber 20.8g
- Total Sugars 7.9g
- Protein 18.1g

Spanish Chickpea Spinach Stew

Preparation time: 10 minutes

Cooking time: 25 minutes

Servings: 4

Ingredients:

- 1 splash olive oil
- 1 small onion, chopped
- 2 cloves garlic
- 5g cumin powder
- 5g smoked paprika
- ¼ teaspoon chili powder
- 235ml water
- 670g can diced tomatoes
- 165g cooked chickpeas (or can chickpeas)
- 60g baby spinach
- Salt, to taste
- A handful of chopped coriander, to garnish
- 20g slivered almonds, to garnish
- 4 slices toasted whole-grain bread, to serve with

Instructions:

1. Heat olive oil in a saucepan over medium-high heat.
2. Add onion and cook until browned, for 7-8 minutes.
3. Add garlic, cumin, paprika, and chili powder.
4. Cook 1 minute.
5. Add water and scrape any browned bits.
6. Add the tomatoes and chickpeas. Season to taste and reduce heat.
7. Simmer the soup for 10 minutes.
8. Stir in spinach and cook 2 minutes.
9. Ladle soup in a bowl. Sprinkle with cilantro and almonds.
10. Serve with toasted bread slices.

Nutritional info per serving:

- Calories 369
- Total Fat 9.7g
- Total Carbohydrate 67.9g
- Dietary Fiber 19.9g
- Total Sugars 13.9g
- Protein 18g

Lentils Bolognese with Soba noodles

Preparation time: 10 minutes

Cooking time: 15 minutes (plus 25 for lentils)

Servings: 4

Ingredients:

Bolognese:

- 100g red lentils
- 1 bay leaf
- Splash of olive oil
- 1 small onion, diced
- 1 large stalk celery, sliced
- 3 cloves garlic, minced
- 230ml tomato sauce or fresh pureed tomatoes
- 60ml red wine or vegetable stock (if you do not like wine)
- 1 tablespoon fresh basil, chopped
- Salt and pepper, to taste

Soba noodles:

- 280g soba noodles

Instructions:

1. Cook the lentils; place lentils and bay leaf in a saucepan.
2. Cover with water, so the water is 2-inches above the lentils.
3. Bring to a boil over medium-high heat.
4. Reduce heat and simmer the lentils for 25 minutes.
5. Drain the lentils and discard the bay leaf.
6. Heat a splash of olive oil in a saucepan.
7. Add onion, and cook 6 minutes.
8. Add celery and cook 2 minutes.
9. Add garlic and cook 2 minutes.
10. Add the tomatoes and wine. Simmer the mixture for 5 minutes.
11. Stir in the lentils and simmer 2 minutes.
12. Remove the Bolognese from the heat and stir in basil.

13. In the meantime, cook the soba noodles according to package directions.
14. Serve noodles with lentils Bolognese.

Nutritional info per serving:

- Calories 353
- Total Fat 0.9g
- Total Carbohydrate 74g
- Dietary Fiber 9g
- Total Sugars 4.2g
- Protein 17.7g

Red Burgers

Preparation time: 10 minutes

Cooking time: 50 minutes

Servings: 4

Ingredients:

Patties:

- 2 large beets, peeled, cubed
- 1 red onion, cut into chunks
- 115g red kidney beans
- 85g red cooked quinoa
- 2 cloves garlic, minced
- 30g almond meal
- 20g ground flax
- 10ml lemon juice
- ½ teaspoon ground cumin
- ½ teaspoon red pepper flakes
- Salt, to taste
- 4 whole-meal burger buns

Tahini Guacamole:

- 1 avocado, pitted, peeled
- 45ml lime juice
- 30g tahini sauce
- 5g chopped coriander

Instructions:

1. Preheat oven to 190C/375F.
2. Toss beet and onion with a splash of olive oil.
3. Season with salt. Bake the beets for 30 minutes.
4. Transfer the beets and onion into a food blender.
5. Add the beans and blend until coarse. You do not want a completely smooth mixture.

6. Stir in quinoa, garlic, almond meal, flax seeds, lemon juice, cumin, and red pepper flakes.
7. Shape the mixture into four patties.
8. Transfer the patties to a baking sheet, lined with parchment paper.
9. Bake the patties 20 minutes, flipping halfway through.
10. In the meantime, make the tahini guac; mash the avocado with lime juice in a bowl.
11. Stir in tahini and coriander. Season to taste.
12. To serve; place the patty in the bun, top with guacamole and serve.

Nutritional info per serving:

- Calories 343
- Total Fat 16.6g
- Total Carbohydrate 49.1g
- Dietary Fiber 14.4g
- Total Sugars 8.1g
- Protein 15g

Hemp Falafel with Tahini Sauce

Preparation time: 10 minutes

Cooking time: 10 minutes

Serves: 6

Ingredients:

- 80g raw hemp hearts
- 4g chopped cilantro
- 4g chopped basil
- 2 cloves garlic, minced
- 2g ground cumin seeds
- 3g chili powder
- 14g flax meal + 30ml filtered water
- Sea salt and pepper, to taste
- Avocado or coconut oil, to fry

Sauce:

- 115g tahini
- 60ml fresh lime juice
- 115ml filtered water
- 30ml extra-virgin olive oil
- Sea salt, to taste
- A good pinch ground cumin seeds

Directions:

1. Mix flax with filtered water in a small bowl.
2. Place aside for 10 minutes.
3. In meantime, combine raw hemp hearts, cilantro, basil, garlic, cumin, chili, and seasonings in a food processor.
4. Process until just comes together. Add the flax seeds mixture and process until finely blended and uniform.
5. Heat approximately 2 tablespoons avocado oil in a skillet. Shape 1 tablespoon mixture into balls and fry for 3-4 minutes or until deep golden brown.

6. Remove from the skillet and place on a plate lined with paper towels.
7. Make the sauce; combine all ingredients in a food blender. Blend until smooth and creamy.
8. Serve falafel with fresh lettuce salad and tahini sauce.

Nutritional info per serving:

- Calories 347
- Total Fat 29.9g
- Total Carbohydrate 7.2g
- Dietary Fiber 4.3g
- Total Sugars 0.2g
- Protein 13.8g

Tempeh Skewers with Dressing

Preparation time: 20 minutes

Cooking time: 10 minutes

Serves: 6

Ingredients:

- 445g tempeh, cut into fingers
- 155ml unsweetened almond milk
- 100g almond flour
- 8g paprika
- 4g garlic powder
- 3g dried basil
- Salt and pepper, to taste
- 15ml olive oil

Finger sauce:

- 60ml melted coconut oil
- 80g hot sauce
- 10 drops Stevia

Dressing:

- 230g vegan mayonnaise
- 115g vegan sour cream
- 1 clove garlic, minced
- 2g chopped dill
- 2g chopped chives
- 1g onion powder
- Salt and pepper, to taste

Directions:

1. Cut the tempeh into slices/fingers. Arrange onto bamboo skewers, soaked in water 30 minutes.

2. Bring a pot of water to a boil. Add tempeh and boil 15 minutes. Drain and place aside.
3. Heat oven to 200C/400F.
4. Pour almond milk into a bowl. Combine almond flour and spices into a separate bowl.
5. Dip the tempeh into almond milk, and coat with the almond flour mixture.
6. Grease baking sheet with coconut oil. Arrange the tempeh fingers onto a baking sheet.
7. Bake the tempeh 10 minutes. In the meantime, make the sauce.
8. Melt coconut oil in a saucepan. Add hot sauce and simmer 5minutes. Add Stevia and remove from the heat.
9. Make the dressing by combining all ingredients together.
10. Toss the tempeh with hot sauce. Serve with prepared dressing.

Nutritional info per serving:

- Calories 351
- Total Fat 29.3g
- Total Carbohydrate 9.9g
- Dietary Fiber 1g
- Total Sugars 0.2g
- Protein 15.5g

White Bean Salad with Spicy Sauce

Preparation time: 15 minutes

Servings: 4

Ingredients:

- 450g can white beans, rinsed, drained or cooked beans
- 1 avocado, peeled, chopped
- 6 cherry tomatoes, quartered
- 1 red onion, thinly sliced

Sauce:

- 80g cashews, soaked in water 4 hours
- 30ml extra-virgin olive oil
- 30ml lemon juice
- 70ml water
- 10g Dijon mustard
- 5g pure maple syrup
- 1 clove garlic
- ½ teaspoon cayenne pepper
- ½ teaspoon paprika powder
- 1 pinch salt

Instructions:

1. Make the sauce; rinse and drain cashews and place in a food processor.
2. Add the remaining ingredients, olive oil, lemon juice, water, mustard, garlic, cayenne, paprika, and salt.
3. Process until smooth and creamy. Place aside.
4. Make the salad; prepared vegetables as described.
5. Toss the beans with avocado, cherry tomatoes, and red onion.
6. Drizzle with prepared dressing and toss once again.
7. Serve or refrigerate before serving.

Nutritional info per serving:

- Calories 366
- Total Fat 24.2g
- Total Carbohydrate 31.9g
- Dietary Fiber 9.5g
- Total Sugars 5.6g
- Protein 11g

Stuffed Sweet Hummus Potatoes

Preparation time: 10 minutes

Cooking time: 15 minutes

Servings: 4

Ingredients:

- 4 large sweet potatoes
- 10ml olive oil
- 200g kale, stems removed, chopped
- 300g can black beans, drained, rinsed
- 240g hummus
- 60ml water
- 5g garlic powder
- Salt and pepper, to taste

Sour cream:

- 100g raw cashews, soaked in water for 4 hours
- 80ml water
- 15ml raw cider vinegar
- 15ml lemon juice
- 1 pinch salt

Instructions:

1. Prick sweet potato with a fork or toothpick all over the surface.
2. Wrap the potato in a damp paper towel and place in a microwave.
3. Microwave the sweet potato 10 minutes or until fork tender.
4. In the meantime, heat olive oil in a skillet.
5. Add kale and cook with a pinch of salt until wilted.
6. Add black beans and cook 2 minutes.
7. Make the sour cream; combine all sour cream ingredients in a food processor.
8. Process until creamy. Chill briefly before serving.
9. Make a slit in each sweet potato.
10. Combine hummus, water, and garlic powder in a bowl.

11. Stuff potato with the kale-bean mixture. Top the sweet potato with hummus and a dollop of sour cream.
12. Serve.

Nutritional info per serving:

- Calories 540
- Total Fat 20.3g   2
- Total Carbohydrate 78.1g
- Dietary Fiber 14.9g
- Total Sugars 3g
- Protein 16.6g

Crusted Tofu Steaks with Caramelized onion

Preparation time: 15 minutes

Cooking time: 45 minutes

Servings: 4

Ingredients:

- 450g tofu, cut into 8 steaks/slices
- 100g graham crackers
- 80g raw cashews
- 230ml unsweetened soy milk
- 120g whole-wheat flour
- 10g garlic powder
- 10g onion powder
- 10g chili powder
- 5g lemon pepper
- 15ml olive oil
- Salt, to taste

Onion:

- 15ml grapeseed oil
- 1 large onion
- 15ml balsamic vinegar
- 15ml lemon juice
- 15ml water
- 15g maple sugar

Instructions:

1. Make the tofu; preheat oven to 200C/400F and line a baking sheet with parchment paper.
2. Combine graham crackers and cashews in a food processor.
3. Process unto coarse crumbs form.
4. Transfer to a large bowl.
5. In a separate bowl, combine flour, garlic and onion powder, chili, and lemon pepper.

6. Pour the soy milk into a third bowl.
7. Coat tofu with flour, dip into milk and finally coat with the graham cracker crumbs.
8. Arrange the tofu steaks onto a baking sheet.
9. Bake the tofu for 15-20 minutes or until golden brown.
10. In the meantime, make the onion; heat grapeseed oil in a skillet.
11. Add onion and cook over medium-high heat for 8 minutes.
12. Add balsamic, lemon juice, and maple sugar. Cook 2 minutes.
13. Add water and reduce heat. Simmer 15 minutes.
14. Serve tofu steaks with caramelized onions.

Nutritional info per serving:

- Calories 617
- Total Fat 29.5g
- Total Carbohydrate 70.6g
- Dietary Fiber 5.8g
- Total Sugars 17g
- Protein 23.6g

Spicy Beans and Rice

Preparation time: 10 minutes

Cooking time: 1 hour 10 minutes

Servings: 6

Ingredients:

- 450g dry red kidney beans, soaked overnight
- 15ml olive oil
- 1 onion, diced
- 1 red bell pepper, seeded, diced
- 1 large stalk celery, sliced
- 4 cloves garlic, minced
- 15ml hot sauce
- 5g paprika
- 2g dried thyme
- 2 g parsley, chopped
- 2 bay leaves
- 900ml vegetable stock
- 280g brown rice
- Salt and pepper, to taste

Instructions:

1. Drain the beans and place aside.
2. Heat olive oil in a saucepot.
3. Add onion and bell pepper. Cook 6 minutes.
4. Add celery and cook 3 minutes.
5. Add garlic, hot sauce, paprika, and thyme. Cook 1 minute.
6. Add the drained beans, bay leaves, and vegetable stock.
7. Bring to a boil, and reduce heat.
8. Simmer the beans for 1 hour 15 minutes or until tender.
9. In the meantime, place rice in a small saucepot. Cover the rice with 4cm water.
10. Season to taste and cook the rice until tender, for 25 minutes.

11. To serve; transfer ¼ of the beans into a food processor. Process until smooth.
12. Combine the processed beans with the remaining beans and ladle into a bowl.
13. Add rice and sprinkle with parsley before serving.

Nutritional info per serving:

- Calories 469
- Total Fat 6g
- Total Carbohydrate 87.5g
- Dietary Fiber 14.2g
- Total Sugars 4.9g
- Protein 21.1g

Chili Quinoa Stuffed Peppers

Preparation time: 15 minutes

Cooking time: 1 hour 5 minutes

Servings: 4

Ingredients:

- 160g quinoa
- 460ml vegetable stock
- 2 red bell peppers, cut in half, seeds and membrane removed
- 2 yellow bell peppers, cut in half, seeds, and membrane removed
- 120g salsa
- 15g nutritional yeast
- 10g chili powder
- 5g cumin powder
- 425g can black beans, rinsed, drained
- 160g fresh corn kernels
- Salt and pepper, to taste
- 1 small avocado, sliced
- 15g chopped cilantro

Instructions:

1. Preheat oven to 190C/375F.
2. Brush the baking sheet with some cooking oil.
3. Combine quinoa and vegetable stock in a saucepan. Bring to a boil.
4. Reduce heat and simmer 20 minutes.
5. Transfer the quinoa to a large bowl.
6. Stir in salsa, nutritional yeast, chili powder, cumin powder, black beans, and corn. Season to taste with salt and pepper.
7. Stuff the bell pepper halves with prepared mixture.
8. Transfer the peppers onto a baking sheet, cover with aluminum foil, and bake for 30 minutes.
9. Increase heat to 200C/400F and bake the peppers for an additional 15 minutes.
10. Serve warm, topped with avocado slices, and chopped cilantro.

Nutritional info per serving:

- Calories 456
- Total Fat 15.4g
- Total Carbohydrate 71.1g
- Dietary Fiber 15.8g
- Total Sugars 8.2g
- Protein 17.4g

Noodles with Peas and Sauce

Preparation time: 10 minutes

Cooking time: 10 minutes

Servings: 4

Ingredients:

- 120g soba noodles
- 250g frozen edamame
- 250g green peas
- 4 carrots, sliced into thin, long strips
- 10g chopped cilantro
- 20g sesame seeds, toasted

Sauce:

- 30ml light soy sauce
- 15ml olive oil
- 30ml lime juice
- 10g sesame seeds
- 10g agave nectar
- 3g chili-garlic paste

Instructions:

1. Make the sauce; place all ingredients in a food blender.
2. Blend 30 seconds, or whisk all ingredients in a small bowl.
3. Cook the soba noodles in a pot with boiling water for 5 minutes.
4. Cook the edamame in a separate pot for 3 minutes. remove the edamame and cook peas and carrots for 30 seconds.
5. Combine warm soba noodles with edamame and peas.
6. Pour over the prepared sauce and toss to combine.
7. Serve.

Nutritional info per serving:

- Calories 341
- Total Fat 10.6g

- Total Carbohydrate 48.5g
- Dietary Fiber 9.6g
- Total Sugars 8.2g
- Protein 20.2g

Gourmet Falafel Bowl

Preparation time: 20 minutes

Cooking time: 10 minutes

Servings: 6

Ingredients:

- 150g cooked brown rice
- 80g cooked quinoa
- 10ml olive oil
- Salt and pepper, to taste
- 1 Roma tomato, chopped
- 1 red onion, diced

Falafel:

- 350g cooked mung beans
- 1 potato, boiled
- 1 tablespoon chickpea flour
- 1 red onion, chopped
- 1 teaspoon grated ginger
- 15ml olive oil

Za'atar tahini:

- 70g tahini
- 45ml lemon juice
- 15ml olive oil
- ½ teaspoon Za'atar spice blend
- Salt and pepper, to taste

Beet hummus:

- 2 large beets, baked, peeled
- 2 tablespoons tahini sauce
- 1 clove garlic, minced
- 50ml lemon juice

- Salt and pepper, to taste

Instructions:

1. Make falafel; combine all ingredients, except the chickpea flour into a food blender. Blend until almost smooth. Stir in chickpea flour and shape the mixture into walnut-size balls.
2. Heat olive oil in a skillet.
3. Fry the falafel until golden brown. 2-3 minutes. Place aside.
4. Make tahini; combine all tahini ingredients into a food blender. Blend until smooth. Place aside.
5. Make beet hummus; toss all ingredients into a food blender. Blend until almost smooth. Season to taste.
6. Assemble; toss quinoa, wild rice, tomato, onion, and olive oil into a bowl. Season to taste.
7. Divide the base among four bowls.
8. Top further with hummus, falafel, and drizzle all with tahini.
9. Serve.

Nutritional info per serving:

- Calories 544
- Total Fat 16.2g
- Total Carbohydrate 80.5g
- Dietary Fiber 15.2g
- Total Sugars 8.8g
- Protein 22.5g

Tofu Vegetable Bowl

Preparation time: 10 minutes

Cooking time: 10 minutes

Servings: 4

Ingredients

- 300g firm tofu drained
- 100g sliced button mushrooms
- 80g sliced bell pepper
- 70g carrot, cut into sticks
- 4 garlic cloves, thinly sliced
- ½ teaspoon crushed red pepper
- ½ teaspoon fresh ground salt
- 80g broccoli florets
- 30ml olive oil
- 2 spring onion, finely chopped
- 1 teaspoon minced ginger

To serve with:

- 200g cooked quinoa
- 30g chopped almonds
- 20g raisins

Instructions:

1. Slice tofu into steaks or cubes and place in a bowl. Drizzle over 15ml olive oil and add ginger. Set aside for 10 minutes.
2. Heat 15ml olive oil over medium-high heat and add onions.
3. Cook onions until soft. Add tofu marinade, mushrooms, and vegetables.
4. Cook, covered for 8-10 minutes or until veggies are tender.
5. Heat a separate skillet over medium-high heat and when hot add tofu steaks.
6. If needed add some more olive oil and cook tofu steaks until nicely golden-brown.

7. Serve while still hot with vegetables, quinoa, raisins, and crushed almonds.

Nutritional info per serving:

- Calories 381
- Total Fat 15.6g
- Total Carbohydrate 46.8g
- Dietary Fiber 6.6g
- Total Sugars 7.1g
- Protein 18.5g

Mexican Bowl with Pico de Galo

Preparation time: 15 minutes + inactive time

Cooking time: 5 minutes

Servings: 6

Ingredients:

- 150g cooked brown rice
- 100g cooked quinoa
- 80g Tofu chorizo, sliced or smoked tofu
- 50g can corn kernels, rinsed, drained
- 15ml olive oil

Pico De Gallo:

- 4 Roma tomatoes, seeded, diced
- ½ white onion, chopped
- 45ml lime juice
- 1 jalapeno pepper, seeded, chopped
- 10g cilantro, chopped
- Salt, to taste

Guacamole:

- 2 ripe avocados, peeled, pitted
- 15ml lime juice
- 30g red onion, minced
- 1 serrano chile, seeded, chopped
- 1 teaspoon chili powder
- 2g cilantro, chopped
- Salt and pepper, to taste

Cashew sour cream:

- 200g raw cashews, soaked overnight
- 150ml water
- 10ml raw cider vinegar

- 10ml lemon juice

Instructions:

1. Make Pico de Palo; combine all ingredients into a bowl. Cover and refrigerate 20 minutes.
2. Make guacamole; mash avocado into a bowl with lemon juice, salt, and pepper. Stir in remaining ingredients. Chill 15 minutes.
3. Make sour cream; drain and rinse cashews. Place the cashews into a food blender. Blend until smooth.
4. Add remaining ingredients and blend until combined. Chill briefly.
5. Heat olive oil in a skillet. Add Tofu chorizo and cook 3-4 minutes. Toss in the brown rice and quinoa. Divide rice mixture among four bowls. Top with Pico de Galo, guacamole, corn, and a dollop of sour cream. Serve.

Nutritional info per serving:

- Calories 563
- Total Fat 34.6g
- Total Carbohydrate 54.8g
- Dietary Fiber 9.4g
- Total Sugars 5.3g
- Protein 17.8g

Purple Buddha Bowl with Eggplant

Preparation time: 30 minutes

Cooking time: 10 minutes

Servings: 6

Ingredients:

- 150g cooked brown rice
- 150g cooked quinoa
- 1 avocado, peeled, pitted, sliced
- 100g can chickpeas, rinsed, drained

Sauce:

- 20 ml olive oil
- 2 shallots, sliced
- 1 tablespoon minced ginger
- 2 cloves garlic, minced
- 2 tablespoons Thai curry paste
- 80ml unsweetened coconut milk
- 45ml light soy sauce
- 120g peanut butter
- 300g eggplant, cubed
- ¼ purple cabbage, shredded
- 20 cherry tomatoes, halved
- 45ml lemon juice
- 1 carrot, sliced
- 40g crushed peanuts
- 1 tablespoon maple sugar
- 2 tablespoons tapioca starch or cornstarch
- Salt and pepper, to taste

Instructions:

1. Heat olive oil in a pan over medium-high heat. Add the cabbage and stir-fry 2 minutes. Remove from the skillet.
2. Heat 1 tablespoon oil in the same skillet.

3. Add shallots, garlic, ginger, and stir-fry until fragrant.
4. Add the curry paste and chickpeas. Cook until very fragrant.
5. Transfer the mixture to a bowl. Stir in peanut butter, soy sauce, lime juice, and maple sugar. Stir to combine. Add coconut milk. Place the cabbage back in the skillet and pour over the coconut milk mixture. Cook 1 minute. Remove from the heat.
6. Coat the eggplant with tapioca starch. Season all with salt and pepper. Heat remaining oil in a clean skillet. Fry eggplant until golden-brown on all sides.
7. Remove to a paper-lined plate.
8. Assemble; in a large bowl, toss wild rice, quinoa, carrot, and cherry tomatoes. Season to taste.
9. Divide among four bowls. Top each with eggplant, cabbage, sliced avocado, and crushed peanuts.

Nutritional info per serving:

- Calories 591
- Total Fat 20.2g
- Total Carbohydrate 64.2g
- Dietary Fiber 14.8g
- Total Sugars 18.6g
- Protein 19.9g

Stuffed Mushrooms with Nut Pate

Preparation time: 10 minutes

Cooking time: 15 minutes

Servings: 4

Ingredients:

- 4 portabella mushrooms caps, stems removed
- 15ml olive oil
- 15ml balsamic vinegar
- Salt and pepper, to taste

Nut pate:

- 140g raw cashew nuts soaked 4 hours
- 15ml coconut aminos
- 1 celery stalk, chopped
- 60g nutritional yeast
- Kosher salt, to taste

Instructions:

1. Heat oven to 190C/ 375F and line a baking sheet with parchment paper.
2. In a bowl, beat olive oil with balsamic vinegar. Brush in mushroom caps with oil mixture and arrange onto a baking sheet.
3. Bake for 15 minutes.
4. In a meantime, make the nut paste; rinse and drain cashew nuts. Place the nuts and celery in a food processor and process until just smooth. In the last seconds of processing, add coconut aminos, nutritional yeast, and salt to taste.
5. Process until the coconut aminos is incorporated.
6. Remove the portabella from the oven and place on a plate. Fill with macadamia pate and serve warm.

Nutritional info per serving:

- Calories 295
- Total Fat 20.1g
- Total Carbohydrate 19.8g
- Dietary Fiber 5.3g
- Total Sugars 2.3g
- Protein 15.5g

Soba Noodles with Tempeh Bacon and Mushroom Sauce

Preparation time: 10 minutes

Cooking time: 10 minutes

Servings: 4

Ingredients:

- 150g soba noodles
- 150g tempeh, sliced
- 15ml coconut aminos
- 10 drops liquid stevia
- 15ml olive oil
- 5g smoked paprika
- 3g ground cumin
- Salt, to taste

Mushrooms sauce:

- 200g mushrooms, quartered
- 15ml olive oil
- 115g unsweetened almond milk
- 20g nutritional yeast
- 10g mustard
- Salt and pepper, to taste

Directions:

1. Make the tempeh bacon; in a bowl, combine coconut aminos, Stevia, 5ml olive oil, smoked paprika, cumin, salt, and pepper.
2. Marinade tempeh 2-3 minutes.
3. Heat remaining oil into a skillet. Cook tempeh for 1-2 minutes per side or until crispy.
4. Lay tempeh onto paper towels and place aside.
5. Make the sauce; heat olive oil into a skillet.
6. Add mushrooms and cook 5-7 minutes or until tender.
7. Transfer the mushrooms to a food blender. Add remaining ingredients and blend until smooth.

8. Cook the soba noodles according to package directions. Drain and combine with mushrooms.
9. Top the noodles with tempeh bacon.
10. Serve.

Nutritional info per serving:

- Calories 323
- Total Fat 9.8g
- Total Carbohydrate 47.3g
- Dietary Fiber 2.6g
- Total Sugars 1.2g
- Protein 18.7g

Dinner Recipes

Polenta with Vegetables

Preparation time: 10 minutes

Cooking time: 40 minutes

Servings: 4

Ingredients:

- 160g polenta
- 700ml water
- 500ml unsweetened almond milk
- Salt, to taste
- 15ml olive oil
- 1 small onion, diced
- 1 red bell pepper, seeded, diced
- ½ green bell pepper, seeded, diced
- 250g can kidney beans, rinsed, drained
- 70g can chop artichoke hearts
- 4 cherry tomatoes, quartered
- 30g nutritional yeast
- 10g almond meal

Instructions:

1. Make the polenta; combine water and almond milk in a saucepan.
2. Bring to a gentle boil.
3. Stir in the polenta, salt to taste, and reduce heat.
4. Cook the polenta, until it thickens and starts to pull away from sides of the saucepan.
5. In the meantime, line baking sheet with parchment paper.
6. Spread the polenta into baking dish. Smooth the top and place aside.
7. Preheat oven to 190C/375F.
8. Heat olive oil in a skillet.
9. Add onion and bell peppers. Cook 7 minutes, stirring gently.

10. Add the beans, artichokes, and tomatoes. Cook 3 minutes.
11. Top the polenta with vegetables and sprinkle with nutritional yeast and almond meal.
12. Bake for 15 minutes.
13. Serve warm.

Nutritional info per serving:

- Calories 350
- Total Fat 8.3g
- Total Carbohydrate 58.9g
- Dietary Fiber 11.2g
- Total Sugars 6.5g
- Protein 13.6g

Asparagus Pea Barley Risotto

Preparation time: 10 minutes

Cooking time: 30 minutes

Servings: 4

Ingredients:

- 220g asparagus spears, trimmed
- 30ml olive oil
- 550ml vegetable stock
- 1 small onion, diced
- 2 cloves garlic, minced
- 1 medium leek, chopped, white part only
- 200g quick-cook barley
- 50ml lemon juice
- 5g lemon zest
- 80g fresh peas
- 80g nutritional yeast
- Salt, to taste

Instructions:

1. Preheat oven to 200C/400F.
2. Drizzle asparagus with 15ml olive oil and place onto baking sheet.
3. Roast the asparagus for 14 minutes. cut into small pieces.
4. In the meantime, bring the stock to a gentle simmer. Keep it warm.
5. Heat remaining olive oil in a saucepot.
6. Add onion and leek and cook 8 minutes.
7. Add garlic and cook 1 minutes.
8. Add barley and toss to coat with oil. Cook 1 minute.
9. Pour in 110ml vegetable stock and cook until absorbed. Continue to add the stock until you have used all.
10. At the last 120ml add peas and remaining stock.
11. Once all the stock is used, remove from heat. Stir in lemon juice, zest, roasted asparagus, and nutritional yeast.
12. Stir gently and season to taste.

13. Serve.

Nutritional info per serving:

- Calories 334
- Total Fat 10.1g
- Total Carbohydrate 55.3g
- Dietary Fiber 12.1g
- Total Sugars 5.3g
- Protein 17.5g

Mediterranean Quiche

Preparation time: 10 minutes

Cooking time: 50 minutes

Servings: 6

Ingredients:

Quiche:

Crust:

- 15g ground flax seed
- 50ml tablespoons water
- 100g almond flour
- 90 oat flour
- 15ml coconut oil
- Salt, to taste

Filling:

- 420g firm tofu, drained
- 40ml unsweetened almond milk
- 2 cloves garlic, minced
- 90g baby spinach
- 55g sun-dried tomatoes, packed in oil, drained, chopped
- 40g nutritional yeast
- 2g dried oregano
- Salt and pepper, to taste

Instructions:

1. Make the quiche; combine ground flax seeds and 2 ½ tablespoons water in a small bowl.
2. Place aside for 5 minutes.
3. Preheat oven to 160C/350F and gently coat 20cm quiche pan with some oil.
4. Combine almond flour, oat flour, and salt in a bowl.

5. Stir in the flax mixture, melted coconut oil, and water. Stir with a spoon until a smooth dough form.
6. Press the dough evenly in the quiche pan, bottom and sides. Poke the bottom few times and cover with a piece of parchment paper. Bake the crust 15 minutes.
7. In the meantime, make the filling; place the tofu and almond milk in a food blender.
8. Blend until smooth. Transfer to a bowl.
9. Heat some oil in a skillet. Add sun-dried tomatoes and garlic. Cook 1 minute.
10. Add spinach and cook gently tossing until wilted.
11. Stir the spinach mixture into the tofu mixture.
12. Stir in the nutritional yeast, basil, and season to taste.
13. Remove the crust from the oven. Fill with prepared tofu-spinach mixture.
14. Bake the quiche for 35 minutes.
15. Remove the quiche from the oven and cool 20 minutes before slicing.
16. Serve quiche with the fresh salad.

Nutritional info per serving:

- Calories 229
- Total Fat 11.3g
- Total Carbohydrate 19g
- Dietary Fiber 5.5g
- Total Sugars 1.1g
- Protein 13.6g

Tomato Glazed Lentils Meatloaf

Preparation time: 10 minutes

Cooking time: 1 hour 30 minutes

Servings: 6

Ingredients:

- 60g tomato paste, no sugar added
- 10g Dijon mustard
- 15ml raw cider vinegar
- 15ml maple syrup
- 15ml coconut aminos or soy sauce, or balsamic vinegar

Meatloaf:

- 200g dried green lentils
- 580ml water
- 15ml olive oil
- 1 small onion, diced
- 1 carrot, grated
- 250g sliced chestnut mushrooms
- 2 cloves garlic, minced
- 60g tomato paste, no sugar added
- 30ml balsamic vinegar or soy sauce
- 135g rolled oats
- 3g dried thyme
- 2g dried basil
- Salt and pepper, to taste

Instructions:

1. Make the glaze; combine all ingredients in a small bowl. Stir and place aside.
2. Make the meatloaf; combine lentils and meatloaf in a saucepan.
3. Bring to a boil.
4. Reduce heat and cook the lentils for 40 minutes.
5. In the meantime, heat olive oil in a skillet.

6. Add onion and carrot. Cook, tossing gently for 5 minutes.
7. Add garlic and cook 1 minute.
8. Add sliced mushrooms and cook 5 minutes.
9. Drain the cooked lentils and place half the lentils into a food blender. Add balsamic, and tomato paste.
10. Add the mushroom mixture and blend until a smooth paste is formed.
11. Transfer the past into a bowl, and fold in the remaining lentils, oats, thyme, and basil.
12. Preheat oven to 190C/375F.
13. Line a meatloaf pan with parchment paper.
14. Pour the lentils mixture into the pan and smooth the top.
15. Bake the meatloaf for 30 minutes. remove from the oven and brush with prepared glaze.
16. Bake an additional 10 minutes.
17. Cool 10 minutes before serving. Slice and serve.

Nutritional info per serving:

- Calories 269
- Total Fat 4.5g
- Total Carbohydrate 45.2g
- Dietary Fiber 14.3g
- Total Sugars 7.1g
- Protein 16.1g

XXL Salad

Preparation time: 20 minutes

Cooking time: 25 minutes

Servings: 6

Ingredients:

Lentils:

- 195g lentils, cooked
- 5ml olive oil
- 10g chopped chives

Mushrooms:

- 225g sliced mushrooms
- 15ml sesame oil
- 15ml light soy sauce
- 60ml vegetable stock
- 1 garlic clove, minced

Zucchinis:

- 3 zucchinis, sliced into thin rounds
- 10ml olive oil
- Salt and pepper, to taste

Tempeh slices:

- 225g sliced tempeh
- 15ml maple syrup
- 15ml olive oil
- 15ml light soy sauce
- ½ teaspoon ground cumin
- 1 pinch cayenne pepper

Dressing:

- 80ml unsweetened soy milk

- 120g vegan mayo
- 5g garlic powder
- 5g dried dill
- 15ml aquafaba – chickpea water
- 15g rice protein powder
- 15g chopped parsley
- Salt and pepper, to taste

Additional:

- ½ head romaine lettuce
- 1 avocado, peeled, sliced

Instructions:

1. Prepare the lentils: cook the lentils and while still warm toss with the olive oil and chives. Place aside.
2. Prepare the zucchinis: toss the zucchinis with olive oil and arrange onto a rimmed baking sheet. Season with salt and pepper, and bake at 180C/350F for 20 minutes, flipping halfway through.
3. Prepare the tempeh: whisk all ingredients together. Add the sliced tempeh and marinate for 15 minutes. Heat the non-stick skillet over medium-high heat. Cook tempeh until brown-crispy, for 2-3 minutes per side.
4. The dressing: combine all ingredients together in a bowl.
5. Assemble layer romaine lettuce in a bowl. Top with lentils, chopped avocado, mushrooms, zucchini, tempeh, and dressing.
6. Serve.

Nutritional info per serving:

- Calories 476
- Total Fat 29.1g
- Total Carbohydrate 36.8g
- Dietary Fiber 14.9g
- Total Sugars 5.2g
- Protein 22.1g

Reuben Tempeh Sandwich

Preparation Time: 5 minutes

Cooking Time: 5 minutes

Servings: 2

Ingredients:

- 150g tempeh, sliced
- 15ml maple syrup
- 15ml tamari sauce
- 2 slices sourdough bread
- 1 tomato, sliced
- ½ avocado, peeled, pitted, sliced
- 4 onion rings
- 150g sauerkraut

Dressing:

- 15g tahini
- 10g peanut butter
- 10ml lemon juice
- 10ml water
- 1 teaspoon chopped chives
- 10ml maple syrup
- 1 pinch paprika

Directions:

1. Prepare the dressing: in a bowl, combine all the ingredients. Place aside.
2. Prepare the sandwich: heat the skillet and add a splash of oil. Add the sliced tempeh, followed by maple syrup and tamari sauce.
3. Cook for 2 minutes per side and remove from the skillet. Add the sauerkraut immediately and cook until warmed.
4. Spread the dressing over toasted bread slices. Starts stacking: place the tempeh on bread, top with tomato, avocado, onion rings, and warm sauerkraut. It is a kind of open sandwich.

5. Serve.

Nutritional info per serving:

- Calories 489
- Total Fat 25.3g
- Total Carbohydrate 49g
- Dietary Fiber 9g
- Total Sugars 12.4g
- Protein 23.7g

Lentil Quinoa Pilaf

Preparation time: 10 minutes

Cooking time: 20 minutes

Servings: 4

Ingredients:

- 195g green lentils
- 150g seitan
- 15ml coconut oil
- ¼ white onion, peeled
- 1 thyme sprig
- 1 garlic clove
- 85g red quinoa
- 400g cauliflower florets, chopped
- 1 sprig thyme
- 1 shallot chopped
- 1 large celery stalk, chopped
- 235ml vegetable stock
- 45g almonds, chopped
- 15g cilantro, chopped
- Salt and pepper, to taste

Instructions:

1. Place the lentils, onion quarter, and thyme in a saucepot. Cover with cold water.
2. Simmer over medium heat until the lentils are tender, for 18-20 minutes. Drain.
3. Meanwhile, heat the coconut oil in a saucepan. Add the shallots and celery and cook for 6-7 minutes. Remove from the skillet. Toss in the cubed seitan and cook until slightly brownish. Remove from the skillet. Place the shallots and celery back in the skillet.
4. Add the quinoa and cook, stirring for 2 minutes. Pour in the vegetable stock and cover. Cook on low until the liquid is absorbed. Place aside, covered, for 5 minutes.

5. Heat the remaining oil in a skillet. Add the cauliflower and cook for 5 minutes.
6. Toss the lentils, quinoa, cauliflower, almonds, and cilantro.
7. Season to taste and serve.

Nutritional info per serving:

- Calories 426
- Total Fat 12.1g
- Total Carbohydrate 53.5g
- Dietary Fiber 21.3g
- Total Sugars 4.9g
- Protein 28.4g

Butternut Squash and Chickpea Pizza

Preparation time: 15 minutes

Cooking time: 40 minutes

Servings: 8 slices

Ingredients:

- 450g butternut squash, cubed
- 2 cloves garlic
- 15ml olive oil, divided
- 15ml maple syrup
- 2g dried thyme
- Salt and pepper, to taste

Pizza:

- 170g whole-wheat pizza dough (store-bought)
- 10ml olive oil
- 280g broccoli, cut into florets
- 1 onion, diced
- 90g can chickpeas, rinsed, drained
- 45g raw cashews
- 5g nutritional yeast
- 2g garlic powder
- Salt, to taste
- 1 red bell pepper, seeded, sliced

Instructions:

1. Preheat oven to 200C/400F.
2. Toss butternut squash, garlic, and thyme with olive oil on a baking sheet.
3. Drizzle the squash with maple syrup and season to taste.
4. Roast the squash for 20 minutes.
5. In the meantime, pull the dough on a round baking sheet to 0.5mm thick.
6. Place the squash in a food blender and blend until smooth.

7. Spread the squash over pizza dough.
8. Heat 10ml olive oil in a skillet. Add onion and broccoli. Cook 3 minutes.
9. Top the butternut squash with broccoli, and chickpeas.
10. In a clean blender, combine war cashews, nutritional yeast, and garlic powder.
11. Process until you have coarse crumbs.
12. Sprinkle the pizza with cashew nuts mixture. Finally, top with sliced bell pepper.
13. Increase oven heat to 220C/425F.
14. Bake the pizza 15-18 minutes.
15. Transfer the pizza onto a wire rack and cool 5 minutes before slicing and serving.

Nutritional info per serving/slice:

- Calories 227
- Total Fat 6.7g
- Total Carbohydrate 36.8g
- Dietary Fiber 6.7g
- Total Sugars 8.2g
- Protein 7.9g

Curry Lentil Spinach Soup

Preparation time: 5 minutes

Cooking time: 40 minutes

Servings: 4

Ingredients:

- 15ml coconut oil
- 1 onion, diced
- 2 cloves garlic, minced
- 10g fresh ginger, minced
- 30g tomato paste, no sugar added
- 15g curry powder
- 950g vegetable stock
- 400ml full-fat coconut milk
- 400g can diced tomatoes
- 290g red lentils
- 60g spinach
- Salt and pepper, to taste

Instructions:

1. Heat coconut oil in a saucepot over medium-high heat.
2. Add onion and cook 5 minutes.
3. Add garlic, ginger, and tomato paste.
4. Cook 2 minutes.
5. Add curry powder and cook 30 seconds.
6. Pour in stock and scrape to remove any browned bits.
7. Stir in coconut milk, diced tomatoes, and red lentils.
8. Bring to a boil.
9. Reduce heat and simmer 30-35 minutes or until lentils are tender.
10. In the last minutes of cooking, stir in spinach.
11. Cook until spinach is wilted.
12. Serve soup warm, with whole-grain bread.

Nutritional info per serving:

- Calories 384
- Total Fat 6.9g
- Total Carbohydrate 60.6g
- Dietary Fiber 28.2g
- Total Sugars 8.9g
- Protein 22.4g

Spicy Bean Balls

Preparation time: 10 minutes

Cooking time: 25 minutes

Servings: 4

Ingredients:

- 420g can black beans, rinsed, drained
- 60g chopped walnuts
- 50g rolled oats
- ¼ red bell pepper, seeded, finely chopped
- 10g chia seeds
- 45ml water
- 30g hot red pepper paste
- 30g light soy sauce
- 5ml sesame seeds oil
- 10g fresh ginger, minced
- 2 cloves garlic, minced

Glaze:

- 45g hot red pepper paste
- 45ml maple syrup
- 45ml rice vinegar or lemon juice
- 20ml light soy sauce
- 15ml sesame seeds oil
- 1 clove garlic, minced

Instructions:

1. Preheat oven to 200C/420F.
2. Combine chia and water in a small bowl. Place aside for 10 minutes.
3. Place the black beans in a bowl.
4. Roughly mash the beans and stir in walnuts, oats, bell pepper, red pepper paste, soy sauce, sesame seeds oil, ginger and garlic.
5. Add chia and stir to combine. Shape the mixture into 2cm balls.

6. Transfer the balls onto baking sheet. Bake for 23-25 minutes.
7. Add salsa and cook 5 minutes.
8. In the meantime, make the glaze; combine all ingredients in a small saucepan. Bring to a simmer.
9. Add in the beanballs and cook 2 minutes.
10. Serve balls warm, topped with glaze.

Nutritional info per serving:

- Calories 372
- Total Fat 12.5g
- Total Carbohydrate 50.2g
- Dietary Fiber 12.9g
- Total Sugars 10.1g
- Protein 16.4g

Tofu Paneer

Preparation time: 5 minutes

Cooking time: 15 minutes

Servings: 4

Ingredients:

- 15g fresh ginger, peeled, cut into small pieces
- 1 onion, peeled, roughly chopped
- 2 cloves garlic
- 280g spinach
- 30ml coconut oil
- 420g firm tofu, drained, cut into 2cm cubes
- 4g turmeric
- 235ml vegetable stock
- 15ml lemon juice
- 3g ground cumin
- 4g garam masala
- 5g chili paste
- 10g coconut sugar
- 80ml full-fat coconut milk
- Salt, to taste
- Naan bread, to serve with

Instructions:

1. Place ginger, onion, garlic, and spinach in a food processor.
2. Process until you have a smooth paste.
3. Heat coconut oil in a large skillet.
4. Add tofu cubes and cook 2 minutes or until gently browned.
5. Sprinkle the tofu with turmeric and toss to coat.
6. Add the spinach mixture to the skillet, along with vegetable stock, lemon juice, cumin, garam masala, chili paste, coconut sugar, and coconut milk.
7. Bring to a boil, and reduce heat.
8. Simmer the paneer for 10 minutes.

9. Remove from the heat and season to taste.
10. Serve with naan bread.

Nutritional info per serving:

- Calories 236
- Total Fat 17.7g
- Total Carbohydrate 13.2g
- Dietary Fiber 4.3g
- Total Sugars 3.9g
- Protein 12.2g

Sweet Potato Poutine

Preparation time: 10 minutes

Cooking time: 25 minutes

Servings: 4

Ingredients:

- 600g sweet potatoes
- 35ml coconut oil
- Salt, to taste

Sauce:

- 30ml coconut oil
- 2 shallots, minced
- 100g cremini mushrooms, chopped
- 80g can chickpeas, rinsed, drained
- 10ml balsamic vinegar
- 15g cornstarch
- 100ml vegetable stock
- 170ml unsweetened almond milk
- 5g nutritional yeast
- 60g raw cashews, chopped
- Salt and pepper, to taste

Instructions:

1. Preheat oven to 200C/420F.
2. Cut potato into matchsticks and drizzle with coconut oil.
3. Spread the sweet potato onto a baking sheet. Bake for 25-30 minutes, tossing halfway through.
4. In the meantime, make the sauce; heat coconut oil in a skillet.
5. Add shallots and cook 3 minutes.
6. Add mushrooms, chickpeas, and balsamic vinegar. Cook 5 minutes.
7. Sprinkle cornstarch over the mushrooms and toss to coat evenly.
8. Whisk in stock and almond milk. Cook until the mixture begins to thicken.

9. Remove the mixture from heat and puree using an immersion blender.
10. Sprinkle with nutritional yeast and cashews.
11. Cook for an additional 2 minutes.
12. Serve potatoes into serving bowls. Pour over prepared sauce.

Nutritional info per serving:

- Calories 404
- Total Fat 17.7g
- Total Carbohydrate 69.1g
- Dietary Fiber 11.6g
- Total Sugars 4.8g
- Protein 11g

Green Pasta

Preparation time: 10 minutes

Cooking time: 10 minutes

Servings: 4

Ingredients:

- 60g fresh basil
- 15ml lemon juice
- 2 cloves garlic
- 40g hemp seeds
- 55ml extra virgin olive oil
- Salt, to taste
- 5g nutritional yeas

Pasta:

- 300g chickpea fusilli pasta
- 4 cherry tomatoes, quartered

Instructions:

1. Cook the pasta according to package directions.
2. In the meantime, make the pesto; combine basil, lemon juice, garlic, hemp seeds, and salt, to taste in a food blender.
3. Blend until smooth.
4. Set the blender speed to low, and drizzle in olive oil.
5. Add nutritional yeast and blend until smooth.
6. Drain the cooked pasta and toss with pesto.
7. Top with cherry tomatoes and serve.

Nutritional info per serving:

- Calories 432
- Total Fat 22.7g
- Total Carbohydrate 44.4g
- Dietary Fiber 11.5g
- Total Sugars 6.7g

- Protein 23.2g

Chickpea Frittata

Preparation time: 10 minutes + inactive time

Cooking time: 30 minutes

Servings: 4

Ingredients:

- 350g broccoli
- 15ml coconut oil
- 225g chickpea flour
- 500ml water
- 2g chili flakes
- 3g thyme, chopped
- 4g lemon zest
- 45ml olive oil
- 10 capers, chopped
- Salt, and pepper, to taste

Instructions:

1. Whisk chickpea flour, and water in a bowl. Cover and refrigerate 2 hours.
2. Preheat oven to 250C/485F.
3. Separate broccoli into florets and toss with coconut oil on a baking sheet.
4. Season the broccoli to taste.
5. Roast the broccoli for 15 minutes.
6. In the meantime, heat olive oil in a cast-iron skillet.
7. Stir chili, lemon zest, and thyme into the chickpea batter. Season to taste with salt and pepper.
8. Once the oil is very hot, pour in the chickpea batter.
9. Gently swirl the batter to cover the bottom.
10. Remove the broccoli from the oven. Top the frittata with broccoli and place back in the oven.
11. Bake the frittata for 10-14 minutes or until deep brown.
12. Remove the frittata from oven and place aside to cool.
13. Top with chopped capers before serving.

Nutritional info per serving:

- Calories 360
- Total Fat 17.9g
- Total Carbohydrate 40.8g
- Dietary Fiber 12.5g
- Total Sugars 7.7g
- Protein 13.5g

Spinach Pancakes with Mushrooms

Preparation time: 10 minutes

Cooking time: 20 minutes

Servings: 4

Ingredients:

- 320g sprouted chickpeas
- 50g spinach
- 160ml water
- 15g cornstarch
- 5g baking powder
- Salt, to taste

Filling:

- 75g raw cashews
- 170ml water
- 1 shallot
- Salt, to taste
- 15ml coconut oil
- 2 cloves garlic, minced
- 200g cremini mushrooms, sliced
- 200g white mushrooms, sliced
- 100g shiitake mushrooms, sliced
- 80g wild mushrooms
- 2 sprigs thyme, chopped

Instructions:

1. Place the chickpeas and spinach in a food blender.
2. Add water, cornstarch, baking powder, and salt, to taste.
3. Blend until smooth. If needed, add more water.
4. Heat some coconut oil in a skillet.
5. Pour 115ml of prepared batter into the skillet. Gently swirl the batter to cover the bottom of skillet.
6. Cook until bubbles appear on the surface.

7. Lift and flip gently. Cook on the other side for 1 minute. Repeat with remaining batter.
8. Place the cashews, water, and shallot in a clean food processor. Process until smooth.
9. Make the mushrooms; heat coconut oil in a skillet.
10. Add garlic and thyme. Cook 1 minute or until fragrant.
11. Toss in the mushrooms and cook 8 minutes.
12. Pour over the cashew sauce and cook 1 minute.
13. Remove from heat.

Nutritional info per serving:

- Calories 275
- Total Fat 13.8g
- Total Carbohydrate 32.7g
- Dietary Fiber 6.4g
- Total Sugars 4.6g
- Protein 10.5g

Mongolian Seitan

Preparation time: 10 minutes

Cooking time: 15 minutes

Servings: 4

Ingredients:

- 10ml coconut oil
- 2 cloves garlic, minced
- 5g fresh ginger, minced
- 1g five spice
- 1g red pepper flakes
- 10ml low-sodium soy sauce
- 100g coconut sugar
- 10g cornstarch
- 30ml water
- 20ml grapeseed oil
- 450g seitan
- 10g sesame seeds
- 2 spring onion, chopped

Instructions:

1. Heat coconut oil in a skillet.
2. Add garlic and ginger. Cook for 1 minute.
3. Add five spice, red pepper flakes and cook 30 seconds.
4. Add soy sauce and coconut sugar. Bring to a boil.
5. Reduce heat and simmer 5 minutes or until the sugar is dissolved.
6. Whisk cornstarch and water in a small bowl. Pour the starch slurry into the skillet.
7. Cook until sauce is gently thickened.
8. In the meantime, heat grapeseed oil in a skillet.
9. Cut seitan in 2cm pieces. Cook the seitan for 5 minutes or until lightly crisp on the edges.
10. Place the seitan in the skillet with prepared sauce. Cook 30 seconds.
11. Remove from heat and divide among four serving bowls.

12. Top with sesame seeds and spring onions.

Nutritional info per serving:

- Calories 275
- Total Fat 5.1g
- Total Carbohydrate 30.1g
- Dietary Fiber 2.1g
- Total Sugars 25.4g
- Protein 25g

Green Amaranth Salad

Preparation time: 10 minutes

Cooking time: 10 minutes

Servings: 2

- 140g dry amaranth
- 45ml lime juice
- 30ml olive oil
- 30g baby spinach
- 15g chopped cilantro
- 1 avocado, peeled, stoned, sliced
- 1 red onion, thinly sliced
- Salt and pepper, to taste

Instructions:

1. Cook the amaranth according to package directions.
2. Toss the warm amaranth with olive oil and lime juice.
3. Allow cooling for 10 minutes.
4. Add spinach, cilantro, avocado, and onion.
5. Season to taste with salt and pepper.
6. Stir gently before serving.

Nutritional info per serving:

- Calories 561
- Total Fat 32.3g
- Total Carbohydrate 61.6g
- Dietary Fiber 14.2g
- Total Sugars 4.3g
- Protein 13.1g

Squash Bean Peanut Stew

Preparation time: 10 minutes

Cooking time: 45 minutes

Servings: 6

Ingredients:

- 420g can black beans
- 30ml peanut oil
- 190g brown rice, cooked
- 3 garlic cloves, chopped
- 400ml tomato sauce
- 4g ground cumin
- 140g peanut butter, smooth
- 1 large onion, onion
- 10g fresh ginger, minced
- 900ml vegetable stock
- 1 chili pepper, finely chopped
- 300g acorn squash, peeled, seeded and cubed
- 25g chopped roasted peanuts
- Salt and pepper, to taste

Directions:

1. Heat the olive oil in saucepot.
2. Add the onions and cook for 15 minutes. Add the ginger and chili; season to taste and cook for 5 minutes stirring.
3. Add the broth, squash, peanut butter, tomato puree, and cover.
4. Cook for 30 minutes over medium heat, or until the squash is tender.
5. Add the beans and cook until heated through.
6. Serve with brown rice and sprinkle with chopped peanuts.

Nutritional info per serving:

- Calories 444
- Total Fat 21.2g
- Total Carbohydrate 56.3g

- Dietary Fiber 8.7g
- Total Sugars 8.3g
- Protein 17g

Vegan Sloppy Joe

Preparation time: 10 minutes

Cooking time: 20 minutes

Servings: 6

Ingredients:

- 780g can chickpeas, rinsed and drained
- 400g can fire roasted tomatoes
- 15ml maple syrup
- 2g dried thyme
- 1 onion, diced
- 5g ground cumin
- 4g smoked paprika
- 5g nutritional yeast
- 2 garlic cloves, minced
- 10ml olive oil
- ½ green bell pepper diced
- 60g organic tomato paste
- 15ml coconut aminos
- 15g Sriracha sauce
- 6 whole-wheat buns

Instructions:

1. Place the chickpeas in a large bowl and mash using a fork.
2. Heat the olive oil in a skillet over medium heat. Add the garlic and onion. Cook, stirring for 4-5 minutes.
3. Add the bell pepper and cook until tender. Add the chickpeas and cook for 2 minutes. Add the remaining ingredients and season to taste.
4. Cook the mixture, stirring for 10-12 minutes or until slightly thickened.
5. Open the buns scoop the mixture onto the buns. Serve immediately

Nutritional info per serving:

- Calories 524
- Total Fat 8.9g
- Total Carbohydrate 89.1g
- Dietary Fiber 24.9g
- Total Sugars 20.4g
- Protein 26.6g

Quinoa Patties with Citrus Sauce

Preparation time: 15 minutes + inactive time

Cooking time: 5 minutes

Servings: 4

Ingredients:

- 15ml olive oil
- 1 small onion, diced
- 1 small celery stalk, diced
- 300g cooked quinoa
- 100g almond flour
- 50g slivered almonds
- 1 tablespoon parsley
- 30g applesauce
- 10g flax seeds
- 25ml water
- Salt and pepper, to taste

Citrus sauce:

- 20ml lemon juice
- 115ml orange juice
- 10g tapioca starch
- 20g red or black currants, mashed
- 5g parsley, chopped

Instructions:

1. Coalmine flax seeds and water in a small bowl. Place aside for 10 minutes.
2. Heat olive oil in a skillet.
3. Add onion and celery. Cook for 5-6 minutes.
4. In a large bowl, combine quinoa, almonds, almond flour, parsley, applesauce, and flax seeds mixture. Season to taste.
5. Stir well until combined.
6. Shape the mixture into 1cm thick patties.
7. Cover with a clean foil and refrigerate 40 minutes.

8. In the meantime, make the sauce; combine all sauce ingredients in a saucepan.
9. Bring to a boil and reduce heat. Simmer for 1 minute.
10. Fry the chilled patties in heated olive oil, until golden.
11. Serve warm with citrus sauce.

Nutritional info per serving:

- Calories 411
- Total Fat 21.5g
- Total Carbohydrate 45.5g
- Dietary Fiber 8.4g
- Total Sugars 8.9g
- Protein 16.5g

Desserts and Snacks

Black Bean Balls

Preparation time: 20 minutes

Servings: 12 balls, 3 per serving

Ingredients:

- 420g can black beans, rinsed
- 80g raw cacao powder
- 30g almond butter
- 15ml maple syrup

Instructions:

1. In a food processor, combine 420g black beans, 60g cacao powder, almond butter, and maple syrup.
2. Process until the mixture is well combined.
3. Shape the mixture into 12 balls.
4. Roll the balls through remaining cacao powder.
5. Place the balls in a refrigerator for 10 minutes.
6. Serve.

Nutritional info per serving:

- Calories 245
- Total Fat 3g
- Total Carbohydrate 41.4g
- Dietary Fiber 17.1g
- Total Sugars 3.1g
- Protein 13.1g

Chia Soy Pudding

Preparation time: 5 minutes + inactive time

Servings: 2

- 45g almond butter
- 15ml maple syrup
- ¼ teaspoon vanilla paste
- 235ml soy milk
- 45g chia seeds
- 1 small banana, sliced
- 10g crushed almonds

Instructions:

1. Combine almond butter, maple syrup, vanilla, and soy milk in a jar.
2. Stir in chia seeds.
3. Cover and refrigerate 3 hours.
4. After 3 hours, open the jar.
5. Top the chia pudding with banana and crushed almonds.
6. Serve.

Nutritional info per serving:

- Calories 298
- Total Fat 13.8g
- Total Carbohydrate 37.2g
- Dietary Fiber 10.8g
- Total Sugars 17.4g
- Protein 10.1g

Blueberry Ice Cream

Preparation time: 10 minutes + inactive time

Servings: 4

Ingredients:

- 140g raw cashews, soaked overnight
- 125g silken tofu
- 230g fresh blueberries
- 5g lemon zest
- 100ml maple syrup
- 100ml coconut oil
- 15g almond butter

Instructions:

1. Rinse and drain cashews.
2. Place the cashews, blueberries, pale syrup, coconut oil, and almond butter in a food processor.
3. Process until smooth.
4. Transfer the mixture into the freezer-friendly container.
5. Cover with a plastic foil and freeze for 4 hours.
6. Remove the ice cream from the fridge 15 minutes before serving.
7. Scoop the ice creams and transfer into a bowl.
8. Serve.

Nutritional info per serving:

- Calories 544
- Total Fat 40.7g
- Total Carbohydrate 43.4g
- Dietary Fiber 2.6g
- Total Sugars 28g
- Protein 8.1g

Chickpea Choco Slices

Preparation time: 10 minutes

Cooking time: 50 minutes

Servings: 12 slices, 2 per serving

Ingredients:

- 400g can chickpeas, rinsed, drained
- 250g almond butter
- 70ml maple syrup
- 15ml vanilla paste
- 1 pinch salt
- 2g baking powder
- 2g baking soda
- 40g vegan chocolate chips

Instructions:

1. Preheat oven to 180C/350F.
2. Grease large baking pan with coconut oil.
3. Combine chickpeas, almond butter, maple syrup, vanilla, salt, baking powder, and baking soda in a food blender.
4. Blend until smooth. Stir in half the chocolate chips-
5. Spread the batter into the prepared baking pan.
6. Sprinkle with reserved chocolate chips.
7. Bake for 45-50 minutes or until an inserted toothpick comes out clean.
8. Cool on a wire rack for 20 minutes. slice and serve.

Nutritional info per serving:

- Calories 426
- Total Fat 27.2g
- Total Carbohydrate 39.2g
- Dietary Fiber 4.9g
- Total Sugars 15.7g
- Protein 10g

Sweet Green Cookies

Preparation time: 10 minutes

Cooking time: 30 minutes

Servings: 12 cookies, 3 per serving

Ingredients:

- 165g green peas
- 80g chopped Medjool dates
- 60g silken tofu, mashed
- 100g almond flour
- 1 teaspoon baking powder
- 12 almonds

Instructions:

1. Preheat oven to 180C/350F.
2. Combine peas and dates in a food processor.
3. Process until the thick paste is formed.
4. Transfer the pea mixture into a bowl. Stir in tofu, almond flour, and baking powder.
5. Shape the mixture into 12 balls.
6. Arrange balls onto baking sheet, lined with parchment paper. Flatten each ball with oiled palm.
7. Insert an almond into each cookie. Bake the cookies for 25-30 minutes or until gently golden.
8. Cool on a wire rack before serving.

Nutritional info per serving:

- Calories 221
- Total Fat 10.3g
- Total Carbohydrate 26.2g
- Dietary Fiber 6g
- Total Sugars 15.1g
- Protein 8.2g

Chocolate Orange Mousse

Preparation time: 10 minutes + inactive time

Servings: 4

Ingredients:

- 450g can black beans, rinsed, drained
- 55g dates, pitted, soaked in water for 15 minutes
- 30ml coconut oil
- 110ml maple syrup
- 60ml soy milk
- 1 orange, zested

Instructions:

1. Place the black bean in a food processor.
2. Add drained dates and process until smooth.
3. Add coconut oil, maple syrup, and soy milk. Process for 1 minute.
4. Finally, stir in lemon zest.
5. Spoon the mixture into four dessert bowls.
6. Chill for 1 hour before serving.

Nutritional info per serving:

- Calories 375
- Total Fat 8g
- Total Carbohydrate 68.5g
- Dietary Fiber 12.1g
- Total Sugars 35.9g
- Protein 11.3g

Easy Mango Tofu Custard

Preparation time: 5 minutes + inactive time

Servings: 2

Ingredients:

- 100g mango puree
- 300g soft tofu
- 15ml lime juice
- 15ml maple syrup

Instructions:

1. Combine all ingredients in a food blender.
2. Blend until creamy.
3. Divide among two serving bowls.
4. Refrigerate 30 minutes.
5. Serve.

Nutritional info per serving:

- Calories 148
- Total Fat 5.8g
- Total Carbohydrate 17g
- Dietary Fiber 1.1g
- Total Sugars 13.9g
- Protein 10.2g

Chickpea Cookie Dough

Preparation time: 10 minutes

Servings: 4

Ingredients:

- 400g can chickpeas, rinsed, drained
- 130g smooth peanut butter
- 10ml vanilla extract
- ½ teaspoon cinnamon
- 10g chia seeds
- 40g quality dark Vegan chocolate chips

Instructions:

1. Drain chickpeas in a colander.
2. Remove the skin from the chickpeas.
3. Place chickpeas, peanut butter, vanilla, cinnamon, and chia in a food blender.
4. Blend until smooth.
5. Stir in chocolate chips and divide among four serving bowls.
6. Serve.

Nutritional info per serving:

- Calories 376
- Total Fat 20.9g
- Total Carbohydrate 37.2g
- Dietary Fiber 7.3g
- Total Sugars 3.3g
- Protein 14.2g

Cacao Thin Mints with Protein Powder

Preparation time: 10 minutes + inactive time

Servings: 10 cookies, 2 per serving

- 60g rice protein powder, chocolate flavor
- 35g cacao powder
- 5ml vanilla extract
- 5ml peppermint extract
- ½ teaspoon liquid stevia
- 90ml melted and cooled coconut oil
- 40g ground almonds

Instructions:

1. Combine protein powder and cacao powder in a bowl.
2. In a separate bowl, combine vanilla, peppermint extract, stevia, and coconut oil.
3. Fold the liquid ingredients into the dry ones. Stir until smooth.
4. Line small cookie sheet with parchment paper.
5. Drop 10 mounds of prepared batter onto the cookie sheet.
6. Sprinkle the cookies with ground almonds.
7. Place in a freezer for 20 minutes or until firm.
8. Serve.

Nutritional info per serving:

- Calories 251
- Total Fat 22g
- Total Carbohydrate 7.1g
- Dietary Fiber 4.3g
- Total Sugars 0.5g
- Protein 12.1g

Banana Bars

Preparation time: 10 minutes

Cooking time: 30 minutes

Servings: 8

Ingredients:

- 130g smooth peanut butter
- 60ml maple syrup
- 1 banana, mashed
- 45ml water
- 15g ground flax seeds
- 95g cooked quinoa
- 25g chia seeds
- 5ml vanilla
- 90g quick cooking oats
- 55g whole-wheat flour
- 5g baking powder
- 5g cinnamon
- 1 pinch salt

Topping:

- 5ml melted coconut oil
- 30g vegan chocolate, chopped

Instructions:

1. Preheat oven to 180C/350F.
2. Line 16cm baking dish with parchment paper.
3. Combine flax seeds and water in a small bowl. Place aside 10 minutes.
4. In a separate bowl, combine peanut butter, maple syrup, and banana. Fold in the flax seeds mixture.
5. Once you have a smooth mixture, stir in quinoa, chia seeds, vanilla extract, oat, whole-wheat flour, baking powder, cinnamon, and salt.
6. Pour the batter into prepared baking dish. Cut into 8 bars.

7. Bake the bars for 30 minutes.
8. In the meantime, make the topping; combine chocolate and coconut oil in a heat-proof bowl. Set over simmering water, until melted.
9. Remove the bars from the oven. Place on a wire rack for 15 minutes to cool.
10. Remove the bars from the baking dish, and drizzle with chocolate topping.
11. Serve.

Nutritional info per serving:

- Calories 278
- Total Fat 11.9g
- Total Carbohydrate 35.5g
- Dietary Fiber 5.8g
- Total Sugars 10.8g
- Protein 9.4g

Banana Cashew Protein Dessert

Preparation Time: 5 minutes + inactive time

Servings: 10 balls, 2 balls per serving

Ingredients:

- 1 ripe banana
- 40g cashew nuts
- 30g chopped dried apricots
- 2 Medjool dates, chopped
- 15g ground flax seeds
- 55g vanilla flavored brown rice protein powder
- 2 tablespoons oatmeal
- ¼ teaspoon vanilla paste

Instructions:

1. Slice the banana into ¾-inch thick slices and microwave on medium for 7 minutes. This step will remove unnecessary liquid.
2. Place the cashews into a food blender. Blend on high until coarsely ground. Add the oatmeal and flax seeds and blend until you have almost fine powder.
3. Add the banana, dates, apricots, and vanilla paste. Blend until you have a sticky dough.
4. Shape the mixture into 10 balls and arrange onto a plate.
5. Refrigerate for 15 minutes before serving.

Nutritional info per serving:

- Calories 133
- Total Fat 4.9g
- Total Carbohydrate 12.6g
- Dietary Fiber 3.1g
- Total Sugars 3.9g
- Protein 10.8g

Pumpkin Pudding

Preparation Time: 5 minutes + inactive time

Servings: 4

Ingredients:

- 470ml soy milk
- 245g organic pumpkin puree
- 30ml maple syrup
- ½ teaspoon cinnamon
- ¼ teaspoon ground ginger
- ¼ teaspoon ground nutmeg
- 55g vanilla flavored brown rice protein powder

Instructions:

1. In a bowl, combine all ingredients, until smooth.
2. Divide between four dessert glasses and chill for 30 minutes before serving.
3. Enjoy.

Nutritional info per serving:

- Calories 163
- Total Fat 2.4g
- Total Carbohydrate 21.8g
- Dietary Fiber 4.1g
- Total Sugars 13g
- Protein 15g

Fast mug Cake

Preparation Time: 5 minutes

Cooking Time: 4 minutes

Servings: 2

Ingredients:

- 25g blanched almond flour
- 30g vanilla flavored brown rice protein powder
- 10g maple sugar
- ½ teaspoon baking soda
- ¼ teaspoon baking powder
- 60ml almond milk
- 10ml melted coconut oil
- ½ teaspoon lemon juice
- 30g fresh blueberries

Instructions:

1. In a large bowl, combine the flour, protein powder, maple sugar, baking soda, and baking powder.
2. Stir in the almond milk, melted coconut, and lemon juice.
3. Fold in the fresh blueberries, without squeezing or crushing.
4. Divide the mixture between two microwave-safe mugs.
5. Microwave the cake for 2 minutes. Remove from the microwave and continue in 30-second intervals, up to 4 minutes, or until the dough is spongy.
6. Serve.

Nutritional info per serving:

- Calories 239
- Total Fat 15.8g
- Total Carbohydrate 12.8g
- Dietary Fiber 3.4g
- Total Sugars 6.8g
- Protein 13.9g

Rich Mango Pudding

Preparation Time: 5 minutes + inactive time

Servings: 6

Ingredients:

- 450g fresh mango
- 115ml full-fat coconut milk
- 110g vanilla flavored vegan protein powder
- 45g chia seeds
- 30ml maple syrup
- 290ml water
- 10ml fresh lime juice

Instructions:

1. Combine all ingredients in a food blender.
2. Blend on high until smooth. Adjust flavor as desired.
3. Divide the mixture between six dessert cups and refrigerate for 30 minutes.
4. Serve after.

Nutritional info per serving:

- Calories 209
- Total Fat 7g
- Total Carbohydrate 22.1g
- Dietary Fiber 3.8g
- Total Sugars 14.6g
- Protein 14.6g

Protein Donuts

Preparation Time: 5 minutes

Cooking Time: 20 minutes

Servings: 10 donuts, 2 per serving

Ingredients:

- 85g coconut flour
- 110g vanilla flavored germinated brown rice protein powder
- 25g almond flour
- 50g maple sugar
- 30ml melted coconut oil
- 8g baking powder
- 115ml soy milk
- ½ teaspoon apple cider vinegar
- ½ teaspoon vanilla paste
- ½ teaspoon cinnamon
- 30ml organic applesauce

Additional:

- 30g powdered coconut sugar
- 10g cinnamon

Directions:

1. In a bowl, combine all the dry ingredients.
2. In a separate bowl, whisk the milk with applesauce, coconut oil, and cider vinegar.
3. Fold the wet ingredients into dry and stir until blended thoroughly.
4. Heat oven to 180C/350F and grease 10-hole donut pan.
5. Spoon the prepared batter into greased donut pan.
6. Bake the donuts for 15-20 minutes.
7. While the donuts are still warm, sprinkle with coconut sugar and cinnamon.
8. Serve warm.

Nutritional info per serving:

- Calories 270
- Total Fat 9.3g
- Total Carbohydrate 28.4g
- Dietary Fiber 10.2g
- Total Sugars 10.1g
- Protein 20.5g

Sweet Hummus

Preparation time: 10 minutes

Servings: 4

Ingredients:

- 60ml vanilla soy milk
- 30ml maple syrup
- 400g can chickpeas, rinsed, drained
- 125g pumpkin puree, organic
- 5ml vanilla extract
- 200g fresh blueberries
- 2 carrots, finely grated

Instructions:

1. Combine soy milk, maple syrup, chickpeas, pumpkin puree, vanilla, and carrots in a food processor.
2. Process until smooth.
3. Serve, topped with fresh blueberries.

Nutritional info per serving:

- Calories 252
- Total Fat 3.1g
- Total Carbohydrate 48g
- Dietary Fiber 10.5g
- Total Sugars 19.2g
- Protein 10.3g

Soft Cacao Ice Cream

Preparation time: 10 minutes

Servings: 2

Ingredients:

- 2 bananas, frozen (slice before freezing)
- 15ml soy milk
- 15g raw cacao powder
- 15g peanut butter
- 5ml maple syrup
- 30g chocolate brown rice protein powder
- 10g cocoa nibs, to garnish
- 20g crushed almonds

Instructions:

1. Combine banana, soy milk, cocoa powder, peanut butter, maple syrup, and protein powder in a food processor.
2. Process until smooth.
3. Divide the ice cream between two serving bowls.
4. Sprinkle with cocoa nibs and crushed almonds
5. Serve.

Nutritional info per serving:

- Calories 297
- Total Fat 11.3g
- Total Carbohydrate 40.6g
- Dietary Fiber 9.3g
- Total Sugars 17.9g
- Protein 18.8g

Lentil Balls

Preparation time: 10 minutes + inactive time

Servings: 16 balls, 2 per serving

Ingredients:

- 150g cooked green lentils
- 10ml coconut oil
- 5g coconut sugar
- 180g quick cooking oats
- 40g unsweetened coconut, shredded
- 40g raw pumpkin seeds
- 110g peanut butter
- 40ml maple syrup

Instructions:

1. Combine all ingredients in a large bowl, as listed.
2. Shape the mixture into 16 balls.
3. Arrange the balls onto a plate, lined with parchment paper.
4. Refrigerate 30 minutes.
5. Serve.

Nutritional info per serving:

- Calories 305
- Total Fat 13.7g   1
- Total Carbohydrate 35.4g
- Dietary Fiber 9.5g
- Total Sugars 6.3g
- Protein 12.6g

Homemade granola

Preparation time: 10 minutes

Cooking time: 24 minutes

Servings: 8

Ingredients:

- 270g rolled oats
- 100g coconut flakes
- 40g pumpkin seeds
- 80g hemp seeds
- 30ml coconut oil
- 70ml maple syrup
- 50g Goji berries

Instructions:

1. Combine all ingredients on a large baking sheet.
2. Preheat oven to 180C/350F.
3. Bake the granola for 12 minutes. Remove from the oven and stir.
4. Bake an additional 12 minutes.
5. Serve at room temperature.

Nutritional info per serving:

- Calories 344
- Total Fat 17.4g
- Total Carbohydrate 39.7g
- Dietary Fiber 5.8g
- Total Sugars 12.9g
- Protein 9.9g

Peanut Butter Quinoa Cups

Preparation time: 10 minutes

Servings: 6

Ingredients:

- 120g puffed quinoa
- 60g smooth peanut butter
- 40g coconut butter
- 30ml coconut oil
- 25ml maple syrup
- 5ml vanilla extract

Instructions:

1. Combine peanut butter, coconut butter, and coconut oil in a microwave-safe bowl.
2. Microwave on high until melted, in 40-second intervals.
3. Stir in the puffed quinoa. Stir gently to combine.
4. Divide the mixture among 12 paper cases.
5. Place in a freezer for 1 hour.
6. Serve.

Nutritional info per serving:

- Calories 231
- Total Fat 14.7g
- Total Carbohydrate 21.2g
- Dietary Fiber 3g
- Total Sugars 4.7g
- Protein 6.3g

Cookie Almond Balls

Preparation time: 15 minutes

Servings: 16 balls, 2 per serving

Ingredients:

- 100g almond meal
- 60g vanilla flavored rice protein powder
- 80g almond butter or any nut butter
- 10 drops Stevia
- 15ml coconut oil
- 15g coconut cream
- 40g vegan chocolate chips

Instructions:

1. Combine almond meal and protein powder in a large bowl.
2. Fold in almond butter, Stevia, coconut oil, and coconut cream.
3. If the mixture is too crumbly, add some water. Fold in chopped chocolate and stir until combined.
4. Shape the mixture into 16 balls.
5. You can additional roll the balls into almond flour.
7. Serve.

Nutritional info per serving:

- Calories 132
- Total Fat 8.4g
- Total Carbohydrate 6.7g
- Dietary Fiber 2.2g
- Total Sugars 3.1g
- Protein 8.1g

Spiced Dutch Cookies

Preparation time: 20 minutes

Cooking time: 8 minutes

Servings: 6

Ingredients:

- 180g almond flour
- 55ml coconut oil, melted
- 60g rice protein powder, vanilla flavor
- 1 banana, mashed
- 40g Chia seeds

Spice mix:

- 15g allspice
- 1 pinch white pepper
- 1 pinch ground coriander seeds
- 1 pinch ground mace

Instructions:

1. Preheat oven to 190C/375F.
2. Soak chia seeds in ½ cup water. Place aside 10 minutes.
3. Mash banana in a large bowl.
4. Fold in almond flour, coconut oil, protein powder, and spice mix.
5. Add soaked chia seeds and stir to combine.
6. Stir until the dough is combined and soft. If needed add 1-2 tablespoons water.
2. Roll the dough to 1cm thick. Cut out cookies.
3. Arrange the cookies onto baking sheet, lined with parchment paper.
4. Bake 7-8 minutes.
5. Serve at room temperature.

Nutritional info per serving:

- Calories 278

- Total Fat 20g
- Total Carbohydrate 13.1g
- Dietary Fiber 5.9g
- Total Sugars 2.4g
- Protein 13.1g

Avocado pudding with Chia

Preparation time: 10 minutes + inactive time

Servings: 4

Ingredients:

- 2 large avocados, peeled, pitted
- 40ml unsweetened cacao
- 45g coconut cream
- 15ml coconut oil, melted
- 30g vanilla flavored rice protein powder
- 4 drops Stevia
- 15g Chia seeds

Instructions:

1. In a food blender, combine avocados, cacao, coconut cream, coconut oil, Vanilla WPI, and Stevia.
2. Blend until smooth.
3. Divide among four serving bowls.
4. Refrigerate 10 minutes.
6. Sprinkle with chia seeds and serve.

Nutritional info per serving:

- Calories 278
- Total Fat 22.6g
- Total Carbohydrate 16.2g
- Dietary Fiber 11.4g
- Total Sugars 0.6g
- Protein 12.1g

Sauces and Dips

Pumpkin Sauce

Preparation time: 5 minutes

Cooking time: 2 minutes

Servings: 6

- 30ml olive oil
- 3 cloves garlic, minced
- 15g cornstarch
- 400g pumpkin puree
- 300ml soy milk
- 45g nutritional yeast

Instructions:

1. Heat olive oil in a saucepan.
2. Add garlic and cook for 2 minutes, over medium-high heat.
3. Add cornstarch and stir to combine.
4. Whisk in soy milk and bring to a boil.
5. Reduce heat and stir in the pumpkin. Simmer for 2 minutes.
6. Stir in nutritional yeast.
7. Remove from heat and serve.

Nutritional info per serving:

- Calories 208
- Total Fat 9.8g
- Total Carbohydrate 20.8g
- Dietary Fiber 4.7g
- Total Sugars 6.7g
- Protein 10.9g

Pasta Sauce

Preparation time: 5 minutes

Cooking time: 10 minutes

Servings: 4

Ingredients:

- 400g can chickpeas, rinsed, drained
- 45ml olive oil
- 1 onion, cut in half
- 3 cloves garlic
- 350ml chickpea water
- 3 sprigs rosemary, chopped
- ½ teaspoon red pepper flakes
- Salt and pepper, to taste

Instructions:

1. Heat olive oil in a saucepan.
2. Add onion and cook 5 minutes.
3. Add garlic and cook 2 minutes, over medium heat.
4. Add chickpeas, chickpea water, rosemary, and red pepper flakes.
5. Simmer for 10 minutes.
6. Transfer the mixture to a food blender.
7. Blend on high until smooth.
8. Serve with pasta.

Nutritional info per serving:

- Calories 394
- Total Fat 17.3g
- Total Carbohydrate 67.2g
- Dietary Fiber 18.9g
- Total Sugars 12g
- Protein 21.2g

Creamy Tofu Sauce

Preparation time: 5 minutes

Servings: 2

Ingredients:

- 350g silken tofu
- 40ml soy milk
- 2 clove garlic
- ¼ teaspoon paprika
- ¼ teaspoon cayenne
- 1 tablespoon dried parsley
- 1 tablespoon dried basil
- Salt and pepper, to taste

Instructions:

1. Toss all ingredients into a food blender.
2. Blend on high until smooth.
3. Serve with pasta or rice.

Nutritional info per serving:

- Calories 127
- Total Fat 5.2g
- Total Carbohydrate 6.9g
- Dietary Fiber 0.6g
- Total Sugars 3.2g
- Protein 13.1g

Spinach Sauce

Preparation time: 5 minutes

Cooking time: 3 minutes

Servings: 2

Ingredients:

- 150g fresh spinach
- 20g fresh basil
- 240ml soy milk
- 5g nutritional yeast
- 15g cornstarch
- 2 cloves garlic
- ½ teaspoon onion powder
- Salt and pepper, to taste
- 1 pinch nutmeg

Instructions:

1. Place all ingredients in a food blender.
2. Blend on high until smooth.
3. Transfer to a saucepot.
4. Bring to a simmer. Cook over medium heat for 3 minutes.
5. Serve warm.

Nutritional info per serving:

- Calories 127
- Total Fat 2.7g
- Total Carbohydrate 19.6g
- Dietary Fiber 3.2g
- Total Sugars 5.3g
- Protein 7.7g

Kidney Bean Sauce

Preparation time: 5 minutes

Cooking time: 8 minutes

Servings: 2

Ingredients:

- 15ml olive oil
- ½ small onion, diced
- 2 cloves garlic, minced
- 400g can red kidney beans, rinsed, drained
- 30ml balsamic vinegar
- 30g tomato paste
- ½ teaspoon cayenne pepper
- ½ teaspoon smoked paprika
- Salt, to taste

Instructions:

1. Heat olive oil in a skillet.
2. Add onion and cook 5 minutes, over medium-high heat.
3. Add garlic and cook 2 minutes.
4. Toss in the beans, balsamic vinegar, tomato paste, and spices.
5. Cook 1 minute.
6. Transfer the mixture to a food blender.
7. Blend on high until smooth.
8. Serve with pasta, falafel, or tacos.

Nutritional info per serving:

- Calories 342
- Total Fat 8.2g
- Total Carbohydrate 51.2g
- Dietary Fiber 15.9g
- Total Sugars 3.3g
- Protein 18.4g

Hemp Alfredo Sauce

Preparation time: 5 minutes

Servings: 4

Ingredients:

- 125g raw cashews, soaked in water for 2 hours
- 80g raw hemp seeds
- 115ml soy milk
- 10g nutritional yeast
- 15ml lemon juice
- 2 cloves garlic, minced
- Salt, to taste

Instructions:

1. Drain the cashews and place in a food processor.
2. Add the remaining ingredients and process on high until smooth.
3. Serve with pasta or soba noodles.

Nutritional info per serving:

- Calories 319
- Total Fat 23.2g
- Total Carbohydrate 17g
- Dietary Fiber 1.7g
- Total Sugars 3.5g
- Protein 13.5g

Vegan Cheese Sauce

Preparation time: 10 minutes

Cooking time: 15 minutes

Servings: 6

Ingredients:

- 450g sweet potatoes, peeled, cubed
- 150g grated carrots
- 100g raw cashews, soaked in water 2 hours, drained
- 65g red lentils, picked, rinsed
- 30g rolled oats
- 20g nutritional yeast
- 30g miso paste
- 15ml lemon juice
- 950ml water
- 10g garlic powder
- Salt, to taste

Instructions:

1. Combine water, potatoes, carrots, cashews, lentils, and oats in a saucepot.
2. Bring to a boil.
3. Reduce heat and simmer 15 minutes.
4. Strain through a fine-mesh sieve. Reserve some of the cooking liquid if you need to thin the sauce.
5. Transfer the cooked ingredients into a food blender.
6. Add nutritional yeast, miso paste, lemon juice, garlic powder, and season to taste.
7. Blend until smooth. If needed, add some cooking liquid to thin down the sauce.
8. Serve with pasta, potatoes, or with poutine.

Nutritional info per serving:

- Calories 278
- Total Fat 8.8g

- Total Carbohydrate 42.6g
- Dietary Fiber 9.2g
- Total Sugars 3.5g
- Protein 9.5g

Pea Cheesy Sauce

Preparation time: 5 minutes

Servings: 2

Ingredients:

- 160g frozen peas, defrosted
- 20 leaves basil
- 30g nutritional yeast
- 30ml lemon juice
- 45ml vegetable stock
- Salt, to taste
- 1 clove garlic

Instructions:

1. Combine all ingredients, except the vegetable stock in a food blender.
2. Blend until smooth.
3. Gradually add in the vegetable stock, until desired consistency is reached.
4. Serve.

Nutritional info per serving:

- Calories 123
- Total Fat 1.5g
- Total Carbohydrate 18.5g
- Dietary Fiber 8.2g
- Total Sugars 4.2g
- Protein 11.7g

Black Bean Lime Dip

Preparation time: 5 minutes

Cooking time: 2 minutes

Servings: 2

Ingredients:

- 2 cloves garlic
- 2cm ginger, peeled, grated
- 400g can black beans, rinsed, drained
- 45ml water
- 15ml olive oil
- 45ml lime juice
- Salt and pepper, to taste

Instructions:

1. Heat olive oil in a skillet.
2. Add garlic and ginger. Cook over medium-high heat until fragrant.
3. Add the black beans and cook 30 seconds. Add water and cook an additional 30 seconds.
4. Season to taste and remove from the heat.
5. Mash the beans using a potato mash. Stir in lime juice.
6. Serve with pita bread or tofu sticks.

Nutritional info per serving:

- Calories 261
- Total Fat 8g
- Total Carbohydrate 39.2g
- Dietary Fiber 9.5g
- Total Sugars 2.1g
- Protein 11.2g

Mediterranean White Bean Dip with Olives

Preparation time: 10 minutes

Servings: 2

Ingredients:

- 400g can white beans, rinsed, drained
- 15g capers, rinsed
- 25g black olives, sliced
- 30ml olive oil
- 30ml lemon juice
- 5g whole-grain mustard
- ½ teaspoon lemon zest
- 2 clove garlic
- 4 basil leaves, chopped
- Salt and pepper, to taste

Instructions:

1. Place white beans in a bowl.
2. Mash the beans using a potato mash.
3. Stir in capers, olives, olive oil, lemon juice, mustard, lemon zest, minced garlic, and chopped basil.
4. Season to taste with salt and pepper.
5. Stir to combine.
6. Chill briefly before serving.

Nutritional info per serving:

- Calories 432
- Total Fat 17.1g
- Total Carbohydrate 54.4g
- Dietary Fiber 21.6g
- Total Sugars 0.4g
- Protein 18.6g

Spinach Artichoke Dip

Preparation time: 10 minutes

Cooking time: 3 minutes

Servings: 6

Ingredients:

- 180g raw cashews, soaked in water for 4 hours, drained
- 15ml olive oil
- 3 cloves garlic, minced
- 300g spinach
- 130ml unsweetened soy milk
- 15ml lime juice
- 150g can artichoke hearts, chopped
- ½ teaspoon cayenne pepper
- ½ teaspoon paprika powder
- Salt and pepper, to taste

Instructions:

1. Heat olive oil in a saucepan.
2. Add garlic and cook until very fragrant, for 1 minute.
3. Add spinach and cook, tossing until wilted.
4. In the meantime, combine cashews, soy milk, lime juice, cayenne pepper, and paprika powder in a food blender.
5. Blend until smooth.
6. Remove the spinach from the heat and allow to cool. Squeeze out the excessive liquid. Stir the spinach and artichokes in the cashew cream.
7. Serve cold or reheat at 180C/350F for 10 minutes.

Nutritional info per serving:

- Calories 231
- Total Fat 17.3g
- Total Carbohydrate 12.5g
- Dietary Fiber 3g

- Total Sugars 2.2g
- Protein 8.1g

Beet Hummus

Preparation time: 10 minutes

Cooking time: 1 hour

Servings: 8

Ingredients:

- 500g cooked chickpeas, drained
- 250g beets, washed
- 180ml cold chickpea water – aquafaba
- 50ml lemon juice
- 2 cloves garlic
- 90g tahini
- 5g ground cumin
- Salt and pepper, to taste

Instructions:

1. Preheat oven to 200C/400F.
2. Wrap beets in a piece of aluminum foil. Arrange the beets on the baking sheet.
3. Bake the beets for 55-60 minutes or until fork tender.
4. Peel the baked beets and chop roughly.
5. Place the chickpea water, lemon juice, garlic, tahini, cumin, beets, and salt and pepper in a food blender.
6. Blend on high until smooth.
7. Serve.

Nutritional info per serving:

- Calories 356
- Total Fat 10.7g
- Total Carbohydrate 51.4g
- Dietary Fiber 14.8g
- Total Sugars 10.7g
- Protein 17g

Fake Crab Dip

Preparation time: 15 minutes

Cooking time: 30 minutes

Servings: 8

Ingredients:

- 120g raw cashews, soaked overnight, drained
- 15ml lemon juice
- 5ml raw cider vinegar
- 400g cooked white beans, drained
- 20g nutritional yeast
- 20g Old Bay Seasoning
- ¼ teaspoon Tabasco sauce
- 280g can heart of palm
- Salt and pepper, to taste

Instructions:

1. Preheat oven to 180C/350F.
2. Combine cashews, lemon juice, and cider vinegar in a food blender.
3. Blend on high until smooth. Transfer to a bowl.
4. Rinse blender.
5. Combine beans, nutritional yeast, Old Bay Seasoning, Tabasco, and drained hearts of palm in a food blender. Blend on high until smooth. Combine the palm heart mixture with the cashews. Transfer to a heat-proof bowl.
6. Bake in heated oven for 30 minutes.
7. Serve warm.

Nutritional info per serving:

- Calories 270
- Total Fat 7.7g
- Total Carbohydrate 37.7g
- Dietary Fiber 9.4g

- Total Sugars 1.9g
- Protein 15.8g

Kale Nut Pesto Dip

Preparation time: 10 minutes

Cooking time: 5 minutes

Servings: 4

Ingredients:

- 300g kale, stems removed
- 60g chopped walnuts
- 2 cloves garlic
- 20g nutritional yeast
- 30ml lemon juice
- 60ml olive oil
- Salt and pepper, to taste

Instructions:

1. Bring a large pot of salted water to a boil.
2. Add kale and reduce heat.
3. Cook the kale for 5 minutes.
4. Drain and rinse under cold water to stop the cooking process.
5. Combine kale, walnuts, garlic, nutritional yeast, lemon juice, salt and pepper in a food blender.
6. Blend on high until smooth.
7. Drizzle in the olive oil and blend until creamy.
8. Serve.

Nutritional info per serving:

- Calories 274
- Total Fat 23.3g
- Total Carbohydrate 12.1g
- Dietary Fiber 3.5g
- Total Sugars 0.4g
- Protein 8.5g

BBQ Dip

Preparation time: 5 minutes

Servings: 4

Ingredients:

- 100g cooked chickpeas, drained
- 90g tahini
- 45g tomato paste
- 5g garlic powder
- 15ml raw cider vinegar
- 15ml maple syrup
- ½ teaspoon smoked paprika
- 1 good pinch chili powder
- 110ml water
- 60ml soy milk

Instructions:

1. Combine all ingredients in a food blender.
2. Blend until smooth.
3. Serve.

Nutritional info per serving:

- Calories 256
- Total Fat 14g
- Total Carbohydrate 26.3g
- Dietary Fiber 7.1g
- Total Sugars 7.1g
- Protein 9.9g

Pea Pistachio Dip

Preparation time: 5 minutes

Cooking time: 3 minutes

Servings: 4

Ingredients:

- 150g frozen peas
- 15g parsley
- ½ teaspoon dried dill weed
- 90g shelled pistachios
- 35ml lime juice
- 55ml water
- Salt, to taste

Instructions:

1. Cook the peas in 4cm water over medium-high heat for 3minutes.
2. Drain and transfer into a food blender.
3. Add the remaining ingredients.
4. Blend on high until smooth.
5. Serve with beanballs, or roasted veggies.

Nutritional info per serving:

- Calories 173
- Total Fat 11g
- Total Carbohydrate 13.2g
- Dietary Fiber 4.7g
- Total Sugars 3.4g
- Protein 7.1g

Lentil Walnut Dip

Preparation time: 10 minutes

Cooking time: 25 minutes

Servings: 6

Ingredients:

- 150g brown lentils
- 90g walnuts
- 10ml olive oil
- 2 shallots, minced
- 2 cloves garlic
- 1 teaspoon dried thyme
- 15ml raw cider vinegar
- 10ml lemon juice
- 110ml water
- Salt and pepper, to taste

Instructions:

1. Place lentils in saucepot. Cover with 2cm water.
2. Bring to a boil.
3. Reduce heat and simmer the lentils for 20 minutes.
4. Drain the lentils and place aside.
5. Heat large skillet over medium-high heat. Add walnuts and dry-toast until fragrant. For 1 minute.
6. Heat olive oil in the same skillet. Add shallots and garlic. Cook 3 minutes.
7. Stir in the lentils, walnuts, and remaining ingredients. Cook 30 seconds.
8. Remove from the heat, and allow to cool. Transfer to a food blender.
9. Blend until smooth.
10. Serve with vegetable crudité or tofu steaks.

Nutritional info per serving:

- Calories 190

- Total Fat 10.7g
- Total Carbohydrate 15.6g
- Dietary Fiber 3.4g
- Total Sugars 0.2g
- Protein 9.4g